CONCILIUM

THEOLOGY IN THE AGE OF RENEWAL

CONCILIUM

CONCILIUM/VOL. 47

CHURCH HISTORY

SACRALIZATION AND SECULARIZATION

edited by ROGER AUBERT

VOLUME 47

CONCILIUM
theology in the age of renewal

PAULIST PRESS
NEW YORK, N.Y./PARAMUS, N.J.

PAULIST PRESS
EXECUTIVE OFFICES: 304 W. 58th Street, New York, N.Y. and 404 Sette
Drive, Paramus, N.J.
Publisher: John A. Carr, C.S.P.

EDITORIAL OFFICES: 304 W. 58th Street, New York, N.Y.
Executive Editor: Kevin A. Lynch, C.S.P.
Managing Editor: Urban P. Intondi

Printed and bound in the United States of America by
Wickersham Printing Co., Lancaster, Pa.

CONTENTS

PREFACE

Anton Weiler/*Nijmegen, Netherlands*

This volume of *Concilium*, with Church history as its basic theme, has been planned as an *interdisciplinary* approach to the problem of secularization, in accordance with the decisions taken at the editors' meeting of 1968. *Concilium* is not essentially historical in nature, but theological. Theology appeals to history in order to clarify present-day theological problems in the light of the past. The members of the editorial committee of the historical section of *Concilium* are fully in agreement with this cooperation. They are convinced that it is essential to renew the problems and methods of history by cooperating with other sciences which can throw light on a given problem. The historian will have to rid himself of his fear of generalization if he wants to avoid isolation by insisting on the so-called *Einmaligkeit* ("once-for-all" character) of the historical individuality of facts and persons. The methodological problem created by such a renewal of history will be examined in next year's volume on Church history.

For the present volume we have asked a psychologist and a sociologist to give us an initial understanding of "secularization" in the development process of the individual and of society. In the *Constitution on the Church in the Modern World* Vatican

Council II described this process as a change in mentality and structures.[1]

In this regard, Fortmann shows that the mentality of the human individual today is very different from that prevailing in the old cultures and their understanding of the "animated" world. Modern man is faced with a world of "facts" which have become neutralized. What does this neutralization or secularization mean sociologically? Laeyendecker, a sociologist, rightly looks for a *broader* orientation than merely pointing to the diminution of the Church's social functions. His general conclusion that "the Christian confession of faith as a legitimizing system was almost identified with the social structures in which it was experienced as meaningful" must be the starting point for the historical questions that are so important for the Church's present self-understanding—namely, how did the supra-empirical legitimation first arise, how did it find expression, and how does it disappear? In an historical analysis this means that we should concentrate on the three dialectic components of a coherent culture: man, the man-made social structures, and the legitimizing systems.

We would have liked to deal with all three, but the individual-psychological approach is still lacking insofar as history is concerned. Therefore, we have concentrated (1) on the structures and the corresponding legitimizing concepts that prevailed in the early Church, medieval Christianity and the post-Tridentine Church, and (2) on internal and external changes that have led to the highly differentiated society of the 20th century.

In this Western European Christian context, Laeyendecker describes secularization as the "loss in social meaning of the Christian supra-empirical definition of reality". But in an historical analysis we must first show how this "Christianity" superseded the (Hellenistic or Roman) religion which prevailed until then and tried to legitimize a new "sacred" answer to the ques-

[1] "Mutatio mentis et structurarum": *Constitution on the Church in the World*, n. 7.

tions about reality as they were then stated. Every's article concentrates on the social determinants that were operative in this process, as well as on the part played by the priest. This latter point is more explicitly dealt with by Meslin who shows how clericalization and sacralization went hand in hand during many centuries of Christianity. This leads to the question whether the institutionalization of the Church did not isolate Christians from the pagan society and priests from the faithful. Meslin maintains that this clericalization increased when the opposition between Church and society was abolished in the Constantinian era.

The "sacralized" community of the medieval Christians enjoyed an astonishing measure of stability because Old Testament and cosmological models held the social-political and ecclesiastical structures in a grip from which it was almost impossible to escape. Congar considers it fatal if a Christian community, which tries to embody the general claims of Christ's message in social structures, refers here to the Jewish and pre-Christian past. It was this which led the medieval Christian community to an intense sacralization expressed in a hundred ways such as the anointing of the king, kingship by the grace of God, church dedications, the ritual place of the priest, the observance of Sunday, tithes, fasts and sexuality. The Christian world simply continued the world of Moses. The Christian people lived just as much under a "sacred law", supported by an increasingly hierocratic regime. On the other hand, this increasing sacralization and clericalization of the Church encouraged the *desacralization* of the profane world. Aristotelianism, with its emphasis on the *natural* origin of the political society, reinforces this. Nevertheless, the principal preoccupation remained centered on the moral goodness of the individual. The theoretical recognition of revolution as an accepted means to abolish an unjust *social situation* was never considered. An all-embracing concept of a sacred order (*ordo*) was the norm, and this led to social fixity, just as taking the past as the norm will hardly excite more than a will-to-reform aimed at a restoration of the past. However, the metaphysical and cosmological anchorage contributed by Scholasticism was affected by the beginnings of secularization through the natural sciences and political thought.

In actual fact, as well as by positive argument, Marsilio of Padua and William of Ockham, and still more Machiavelli, inaugurated the modern State. Bornewasser describes the secularization process in State and politics from the Renaissance to the French Revolution. We wanted to stress these "worldly" developments because Church history cannot be understood once it is detached and isolated from the general context. Here one is struck again by the way in which new structures look for new legitimations. It is particularly important to see how the (quasi-) religious considerations are driven out of political theory, and how rational, practical thought begins to prevail. In spite of this, the absolute kingship of "divine right" is still adorned in sacred garments. No one will be astonished that in this ambiguous process the role of the great reformers remains ambiguous itself: the great figures of the second period of Scholasticism are in the same position.

The theorists of natural law and the physicists had a far more immediate impact, but, according to Dussel, this secularization of science led in the end to a—highly unacceptable—secularism. The identification of the Christian faith with a particular culture which developed through historical circumstances was also a misconception that would come home to roost. Julia and Frijoff show how the priest reacted to this secularization by clericalization. His image is deliberately *different* from that of the layman, as being raised above worldly affairs, from which he also cuts himself off in the cultural sense by limiting himself to what is "religious". Only after the sharp rift between clericals and anticlericals was overcome by the much deeper distinction between Christians and non-Christians did the priest find his way back among the people from whom he had become alienated by a centuries-old process.

Comblin then examines the present worry about the reaction of the priest and the institutional Church to the changes that

have taken place in society. The editors did not think it responsible to give the readers only an historical analysis of the secularization process without also giving them a critical evaluation in
the light of the Gospel. In a penetrating manner, Comblin
shows how the pre-conciliar Church rejected this process, and
he then indicates the ways in which the new theology seeks to
recognize the particular values and dynamism of the world: the
Church no longer seeks to dominate but rather to serve the
world. The author points, however, to the element of mystification hidden in this process: the danger of reducing Christianity to a Hegelian idealistic view of religion, the spirit and
history, and here sociological-religious research seems to support
the (idealistic) theory in its concentration on the actual development and causes of secularization. Thus today Christianity
seems to be "accepted" if it keeps in step with the rhythm of
history, which does away with uncertainty or despair. Comblin's basic objections to the theory of secularization deny the
radical character of the changes observed: there has only been
a shift from the sacred to the secular. Man is and remains both
secular and religious: the new civilization only shows new forms
of the sacred. This is only a matter of redrawing the boundaries,
and this is demanded by the new urban and industrial society
which has definitely thrown the old social-political structures
overboard. An optimistic certainty, based on the myth of
secularization which makes us think that history will bring
us the "true" Christianity, conceals the spiritual weakness which
besets the post-conciliar period.

Should we perhaps listen to the Christian East, where people
think themselves protected against an internal secularization
process by their *own* concept of the Church as "communion
with divine life" and by their *own* view of Christian existence
as the "progressive transformation of mankind into the likeness of the risen Christ"? Dalmais shows, however, that both
the structures of the Eastern Churches and their concept of
man's relation to God are profoundly influenced by a pre-
Christian idea of the sacred, which found such prominent ex-

pression in the Byzantine emperor's cult. The key words to an understanding of the situation in the Christian East are Byzantine culture, sacralization and isolation. But there only a few dare to timidly ask what the lasting value may be of this Byzantine view of the sacred for orthodoxy, particularly in a world dominated by an officially atheistic ideology and making intense progress in technological development.

The situation in East and West is too different, too determined by specific cultural and historical factors, to provide us with a common answer to the alleged "spiritual weakness". We need more dialogue research.

PART I
ARTICLES

PART 1

ARTICLES

Leonardus Laeyendecker/*Amsterdam, Netherlands*

The Sociological Approach
to Secularization

A sociological approach to the phenomena that are gathered under headings such as secularization, sacralization and desacralization runs into various difficulties.

First of all, there is confusion about terms and notions, and the meanings given to these by different authors show little convergence. It is becoming clear, moreover, that the usage of these terms and notions is linked with traditional Christian views about religion and Church. Few have attempted to open up new perspectives in this field.[1]

This orientation can also be traced in the various sociological investigations carried out on these problems. Usually sociologists have understandably and not wholly unjustifiably approached the process of secularization mainly in terms of diminished attachment to the institutional Church. Consequently, we have a fair number of studies about ecclesiastical participation but practically none about the wider problems.[2]

Finally, in this field sociological thought is closely linked with other disciplines, particularly philosophical anthropology and theology. If it is already difficult in general to avoid philosophical considerations in empirical sociology, here they play a very important part. And this means that here empiricism cannot have the last word.

[1] For more details, see A. J. Nijk, *Secularisatie* (Rotterdam, 1968).
[2] This is connected with the limitation of theoretical orientation.

9

If I attempt here to point to some fundamental connections, the reader should remember what has just been said, in the sense that what follows presupposes a philosophical choice, the viability of which has not yet been satisfactorily proven.[3]

Social Reality Is Man-Made

At birth man is already surrounded by a number of institutions and by a conduct prescribed by society. Though biologically marked by great plasticity, man is culturally formed by a process of education that ultimately leaves no practical distinction between nature and culture. The growth of the personality takes place in society.

As far as our knowledge of human history can reach back, we can observe the presence of institutions. It is empirically impossible to find out how they originated. Any discussion about their origin is therefore strictly speculative. Our knowledge of the dynamics of institutions and the process of institutionalization is based on an analysis of actual reality. This knowledge can be used in our description and explanation of the past insofar as we know it. What does this analysis show us?

In the process of institutionalization, man's thought and action are molded into more or less stable patterns of thought and action. In a certain sense these patterns gradually begin to develop an independent existence and to react upon man with a certain compulsion. They are, in Durkheim's words, external to man and assume an obligatory character.[4] However, we must avoid turning them into independent things because these objective forms originate in and continue to exist in virtue of the subjective actions of individuals. They can only be seen as a living

[3] I have relied mainly on T. Luckmann, *Das Problem der Religion in der modernen Gesellschaft* (Freiburg i. B., 1963); P. L. Berger and T. Luckmann, *The Social Construction of Reality* (New York, ²1967); P. L. Berger, *The Sacred Canopy* (New York, 1967).

[4] E. Durkheim, *Les règles de la méthode sociologique* (Paris, ¹⁵1963), pp. 3-15; R. F. Beerling, *Wijsgerig sociologische verkenningen* I (Arnhem, 1964), pp. 129-217.

reality in terms of individual actions and only exist insofar as individuals act in conformity with these patterns.

That men act as they do has a definite meaning. No other presupposition can serve as a starting point for human sciences. This meaning is defined by man himself and is expressed in language, which is the most fundamental of all institutions. This language, like other words, is the product of human activity and makes this activity possible. It is both the product and the means of communication. Just because language makes it possible to communicate meaning, we can construct this process of giving human meaning to things as an objective reality. And so the world of human experience is arranged in a meaningful order.

Our ways of thinking and acting, socially prescribed and experienced and maintained as meaningful, are related to every sphere of life. Their duration and power can be either limited or long-lasting and fundamental. In the latter case, they center mainly around the key aspects of man's life: birth, death, education, man's lot and man's destiny. In between there lies a multiplicity of degrees and nuances. We can also group institutions into institutional sectors: political, economic, religious and family institutions, and so on.

The process of institutionalization includes legitimation, understood as the explanation and justification of institutional activity.[5] Here we can distinguish several levels. A beginning of this legitimizing process is found in the system of linguistic objectification, at the level of: This is the way in which things are done. A second level shows rudimentary theoretical statements in the form of proverbs, sayings, legends and folklore. A third level might be that of more specialized sets of knowledge formulated in relation to institutional sectors. At the highest level we find those views or philosophies of life which embrace all human activity and have the widest scope. The history of society and that of individuals have a "meaningful" place within

[5] Berger and Luckmann, *op. cit.*, pp. 92f.

these legitimizing processes, particularly in connection with borderline situations.

This legitimizing process consists of cognitive and normative elements, ideas about what is and what ought to be. It implies therefore a given definition of reality which can be related to either particular sectors or to the whole of reality.

The development of this legitimizing process also implies objectification. Moreover, it creates a kind of sedimentary knowledge and consequently an accumulation of knowledge. This knowledge makes it possible to discern various degrees of co-ordination into rational systems—for instance, pre-scientific and scientific knowledge. These systems of legitimation also have an existence, more or less independent of individuals. But they only have social value if and insofar as they are what Weber [6] calls Träger ("carriers")—in other words, if and insofar as they are actually embodied in the thought and activity of individuals. And this is only possible when these legitimizing systems have meaning for those concerned in their concrete situation in life. In plain words: a norm will be obeyed as long as it makes sense. When it becomes meaningless, it is abandoned and no longer has any sociological value.[7]

The systems of legitimation therefore presuppose people, groups, relationships and processes. All this taken together is called the social infrastructure by Berger and Luckmann, and in a sense this functions at the same time as the structure of a systems credibility.[8] This means that people keep such a system alive in their social relationships by maintaining its reality, its objectivity, in their mutual relations. This too takes place at various levels—for instance, in a very simple way by continuing to act within the legitimized institutions or, very formally, by adhering to official declarations in such matters. In this latter case those whose function it is to maintain the definition of

[6] M. Weber, *Wirtschaft und Gesellschaft* (Cologne/Berlin, ⁵1964), pp. 368-405.

[7] This only holds with a certain limitation. It is possible to maintain norms by the use of power.

[8] Berger and Luckmann, *op. cit.*, pp. 92f.

reality as expressed in these systems play an important part. This function can in turn be officially recognized, and so a new element arises within the institutionalized and legitimized pattern.

Such a view therefore shows a dialectic relationship between persons, social structures and legitimizing systems. They all depend on each other, even though tensions may exist. This means that changes in one sector do not necessarily lead to changes in another. More specifically, it means that the social reality in all its aspects is a product of human society. Prescribed ways of acting and cognitive and normative ideas arise from the interaction of people upon each other. With regard to the cognitive and normative ideas we may say that they are necessarily determined by society. This holds also for what can be called religious ideas.

The Christian Definition of Reality

When we bring in the notion of religion, we touch on a key problem in the matter of secularization. For the question is *where* in the above argument religion has a place and what in that case must be considered the essential element.

On this point there is, of course, no agreement. The difference lies above all in the question whether every philosophy of life in the above sense must be called "religion" or only those views which include a reference to some "supra-empirical reality".[9] In Western linguistic currency religion is practically always taken in the latter sense. Within this context the notion of "Church" is also of importance if understood as a philosophy of life with its corresponding social infrastructure. In other words, in Western linguistic usage religion has a theistic, dualistic and ecclesio-centric character.[10]

[9] Cf. J. M. Yinger, *Religion, Society and the Individual* (New York, ²1960), pp. 7-17; C. Y. Glock and R. Stark, *Religion and Society in Tension* (Chicago, 1965), pp. 3-17.

[10] P. H. Vrijhof, "De religieuze personalisatie als centraal probleem van de godsdienst sociologie," in *Sociale Wetenschappen* 8 (1965), pp. 157-75.

If we take religion as a specific definition of reality and consider it here in the shape of Christianity, leaving aside for the moment its internal variations, we can say that in the past the Church has concentrated on keeping this specific definition of reality alive. She has given a concrete expression to this definition through a complicated set of dogmatic propositions, rules of behavior, forms of ritual and organizational structures which provided her members with a pattern of interpretation and orientation required for their personal life. This definition could remain alive as long as it was meaningful in practice and experience for the concrete situation within which they had to act. In other words, the Christian confession as a legitimizing system was very closely bound up with the social structures within which it was experienced as meaningful. On the one hand, the specific confession was carried and propped up by the social structures; on the other hand, it legitimized these same structures, and the emphasis was bound to fall on the sanctioning and stabilizing effect of this legitimation. Because—and to the degree that— this interpretation (cognitive and normative) referred to a supra-empirical, intangible and model reality, the social reality was made to share in all this.

Here we have to face two very serious questions. The first is: How, as a result of what, and under which conditions did this supra-empirical legitimation first arise, and is it still active? The second is: How, as a result of what, and under which conditions does it disappear?

As in the case of the original forms of institutionalism, any statements about the primordial, hardly articulate, supra-empirical legitimations can only be speculative. The most ancient, prehistoric indications already show a later phase of development: they point to preoccupation with death and man's destiny.[11] On the basis of later and more data, Eliade concluded hat "reality was closely connected for primitive man with a heavenly archetype".[12] Viewed in this light, Jewish-Christian thought

[11] E. O. James, *Prehistoric religion* (London, 1957).
[12] M. Eliade, *Le mythe de l'éternel retour* (Paris, 1949).

is on the one hand a continuation of this orientation, and, on the other, a profound modification of it, because the biblical definition of reality rests on the idea of one, almighty, free and creating God.[13] We therefore do not know of man otherwise than already in possession of supra-empirical legitimations. And if the origin is hidden in the inaccessible darkness of the absolute past, all we can do is to try to find an answer to the second part of the first question. But in my opinion, this is closely linked with the answer to the second question: How, as a result of what and under which conditions does the supra-empirical legitimation disappear?

The Processes of Change

In this survey of fundamental relations, it is impossible to answer this question in detail. We would also be seriously handicapped by the lack of research. But if we start from the considerations developed above, we can situate the factors which play a part in the process of change in the three key points of this dialectic complex—namely, the social structures, the legitimizing systems themselves and man in his actual condition. Changes in any of these points inevitably bring about changes in the other ones, though not necessarily at once. These processes of change interact upon each other, which makes it impossible to explain them by any single cause. It is not possible to proceed otherwise than by analytical distinctions. Changes in social structures are more acute in one period than in another. They are usually described in global terms at the broadest level, and must therefore be given a more accurate concrete expression for every region and every age. These global terms, which ultimately provide less insight than appears, are, among other things, the development of the money economy, the development of trade, the breakdown of feudal attitudes toward authority, industrialization, migration and urbanization, democratization of education, the increase in vertical social mobility, and the develop-

[13] F. Gogarten, *Verhängnis und Hoffnung* (Munich/Hamburg, 1966).

ment of modern means of communication. All these are aspects of a process which can be described in still more general terms as the development of a highly differentiated society which destroys the unity of the social infrastructure. We are seeing the rise of social segmentation and a plurality of societies. This makes it impossible, and inevitably so, to maintain one particular definition of reality as the exclusive vehicle of salvation. People live in different social worlds, with quite distinct cognitive and normative orientations which can be in conflict with each other or at least show up the relative character of each. Moreover, the traditional definition of reality is becoming constantly less meaningful for an existential situation that has been fundamentally modified and as a result is losing its social value.

It looks very much as if the significance of changes in social structure for changes in the legitimizing systems (here: religion, and, specifically Christianity) has received little attention, compared with the historical changes in our concepts.

On this last point, the most striking aspect is the significance of the growth of the various sciences. Here it is useful to distinguish between natural and human sciences. The development of the natural sciences leads to a diminution of the sphere of non-physical causes and to the autonomy of the natural processes. In this field there has been strong resistance (Galileo, Darwin), but at present this autonomy of the scientific interpretations of the physical world is pretty generally accepted.[14] The case of the human sciences is far more problematic because these sciences have direct implications for the manner in which we define man, and this makes the confrontation with the traditional Christian image of man inevitable and painful. At the theoretical level this is already clear in the view of man and his world as based on the results achieved by the human sciences mentioned above. In practice it confronts us daily in the problems affecting Christian moral conduct (natural law, eternal norms, etc.). In this development the scientific findings concerning the great cul-

---

[14] With the exception of fundamentalist tendencies.

tural differentiation, the basic malleability of the newborn individual and the way norms develop are of great importance.[15]

What we call secularization today can be described as the
loss in social significance of the Christian supra-empirical definition of reality. This is clear in, among other things, the reduc-
tion of the meaning and influence of the Christian Churches
which try to preserve this definition of reality.[16]

It might be thought obvious that an analysis of the factors
which play a part in the process of secularization is in fact an
investigation of the processes of social-cultural change. However,
the difficulty is that, in curious contrast with the importance
of this question, this investigation has hardly got off the ground,
both theoretically and empirically. This makes it easy to remain
stuck in general formulas which, for lack of specification, can
hardly be tested. This applies even more to a process of such
depth and scope as the process of secularization. This is also
shown by the divergent opinions and statements concerning the
problem of how far this process has already developed and how
far it will continue to develop.

The Present Situation and Prognosis

The replies to the question as to how far the secularizing
process has advanced are more assertive than persuasive. The
available data indeed show a diminishing ecclesiastical participation, but this is really secondary. What is more important is
how far people's personal and social life is still defined in supra-
empirical terms. In private life there are still so many firm con-
victions about a personal and caring God that to speak about
modern man as secularized is rather glib. It looks as if this process is far more advanced in social life, although it is far from
completed. This is most strikingly illustrated by the increased

[15] These arise mainly from sociological and cultural-anthropological
research by E. Durkheim, G. H. Mead, R. Benedict, A. Kardiner and
others.

[16] The same development can be observed, *mutatis mutandis*, in other
religions.

changeability of the patterns of social life. Here Howard Becker deserves to be mentioned. He approached the process of secularization in terms of a readiness to accept changes. This view is understandable in the light of the study of legitimation and may well prove viable in sociological research.[17] However, one should remember that all institutionalization and legitimation imply resistance to change and that the resistance rooted in a supra-empirical legitimation is but a special form which in specified research must be distinguished from other kinds of resistance, and this really brings us back to the problem in another form. In brief: there are, no doubt, many indications of a secularization process which has advanced in various degrees within various sectors of society, but we have not yet reached the stage where accurate statements can be made.

The question of how far this process can continue is still more difficult to answer. In the sphere of private life we are faced with the problem of the ultimate questions—for example, about suffering and death—which always require an answer. Any answer to the question of how far this answer can, will or must be supra-empirical differs little from an expression of faith. It is, in any case, beyond sociological judgment. But this also makes it difficult to make any pronouncements in the social sphere, because those ultimate questions are not purely private but have important consequences for social life. It should therefore be obvious that a prognosis of the further development of secularization and its eventual final stage simply cannot be made satisfactorily at present. The available data do not allow it.

Finally, we must point out that how far supra-empirical legitimations can still arise even now depends also on these developments. It is obviously impossible to prove that this is not possible, but here, too, our data are too meager to allow a careful specification of circumstances and conditions.

---

[17] H. Becker, "Current Sacred-Secular Theory and Its Development," in H. Becker and A. Boskoff, *Modern Sociology in Continuity and Change* (New York, 1957), pp. 133-85.

A fundamental issue is what far-reaching consequences the disappearance of supra-empirical legitimations will have for Christianity. In other words: How far is the traditional definition of reality a *conditio sine qua non* for a genuine Christian confession of faith? The sociologist cannot answer this question, although he may be forced to ask it on the grounds of what has been said above. Here he must refer to other authors.[18]

[18] See Nijk, *op. cit.*, Luckmann, *op. cit.*, and Berger, *op. cit.*

Henricus Fortmann/*Nijmegen, Netherlands*

Primitive Man:
The Poet and
the Believer

In his profound and rich but difficult book *Urmensch und Spätkultur* (*Primitive Man and Modern Culture*, Bonn, 1956, p. 119), Arnold Gehlen says that it is practically impossible for modern man to really understand the pre-Christian cultures, because our society is "worlds" away from that of the ancient cultures, and not even so much in time as in plain quality.

This may sound exaggerated, but one soon discovers that there are good grounds for such a view when we consider how many ways of thinking that were obvious for ancient man have simply become impossible for us. We simply cannot see a goddess in the moon—and this not only since Lovell's Christmas journey. Nor can we see more than a fairy tale in an Indian story from Columbia which begins like this: "A boy and a girl went into a forest and began to fast in order that they might soon learn the language of the owls" (Gehlen, p. 133). Today if Boy Scouts or Brownies go into the woods to study the life of the owl, they don't have to fast. And while the owl may still always have something mysterious about it for poetical natures because of its wide-open eyes and the soundless beat of its wings, it nevertheless remains an owl and nothing but an owl, a mighty interesting creature, but all the same an object of study. It is an object that can be studied; its habits can be observed, cataloged

21

and photographed. It no longer "refers" to another, equally real but invisible and not quite natural world, as it did for the Indians.

What, then, has happened to the moon and the owls and the whole visible world? Nothing in particular. But something has happened to man. His relation to the visible world is changed. This change can be described either by describing man himself or by describing what this world looks like today to us—that is, to people of this age. For we get to know man by studying the world as he sees it—or, rather, makes it. The decisive factor in this change is that for ancient man the landscape was "animated", both the cover and revelation of invisible powers which could be called "supernatural" on condition that this word means something different from what it means in Christian theology. In the mind of the ancient peoples the "supernatural" is "of this world", though invisible, dangerous or at least incalculable. It shows itself where something striking or out of the ordinary disturbs the daily round of events. You have to watch out if a black crow comes swooping down from your left. Whole cultures were based on this kind of "supernatural" manifestation. In establishing its power, the Roman Empire was always guided by augurs and auspices, and in this way generals were instructed how to cope with these capricious numinous powers. There was no need to "believe" in these numinous powers, because they were daily experienced as a reality. It is true that among the people some were more rationally inclined and others more religiously (P. Radin), but, as a whole, ancient society took the "supernatural" very seriously and as a matter of course.

Our world, however, is neutral, a framework for research. It no longer stimulates timidity and reverence, but curiosity. It has changed in quality. The moon is just itself, a landscape of chalk and craters. The outer world is no longer loaded with an "other" reality. It has become a chain of "facts". And facts are there to be investigated in their causes and reactions. The first Russian spaceman said on his return that he did not see any God. And he spoke the truth because he was looking for something else.

But what, then, moved Lovell to read the narrative of Genesis

I in his space cabin? More precisely: How *could* he still do it without getting into conflict with himself? How could an explorer suddenly become so archaic?

The monotheism of the Bible caused the world of the old religions to crack wide open. The same thing had already happened in the philosophy of the pre-Socratic thinkers. To describe this event we use various words which all come down to the same thing: secularization, demythologization, disenchantment, neutralization. The numinous is no longer the hidden, extraordinary, unpredictable and dangerous aspect of earthly things. It is no longer on "this side" (*diesseitig*) as the old gods and goddesses were. The divine is above, not within, things. This "above" must not be understood in space but existentially, as Augustine in his *Confessions* saw the divine light "above himself": "Not as the oil drifts on top of the water, or as the sky is above the earth: the light was 'above' me because it had made me and I was below because I was made by the light" (7, X, 16).

When this view penetrates, the earth becomes definitely neutral; it is "secularized". No wonder that doubt begins to surround the divinity itself. The pre-Socratic thinkers did not find God (at least not in their natural philosophy), no more than Gagarin. Monotheism and science, turning the world into an object, seem to have deprived man of a vital way of knowledge through which the people of the ancient world saw more *in* things than the real nature of these things. If there is a God, he is "distant", "above". The world itself consists of facts, just as man finds facts *in* himself. And so we have an external world of facts and an internal world of facts (Gehlen) that are there to be investigated.

Yet this process of secularization took a long time to mature. One cannot simply impose a new structure on the human consciousness. The old norms and standards persisted for a long time (Köhler; see Gehlen, p. 22). The gods were replaced by miracle-working saints, holy wells and holy wounds gave rise to places of pilgrimage, and to this very day astrology still holds its own.

Obviously, those saints were not to be called gods. Both Rome and the Reformation objected to that. Nevertheless, the history of Catholic Christianity is one vast effort to keep the distant God in the vicinity. The simple people did that in the way the great ones among the pagans did it. In the northern countries we may say that this effort has by now been broken. From Erasmus and the philosophers of the Enlightenment onward this archaic mentality suffered one defeat after another. The Bible (in its essence), the Church leaders (in their more enlightened moments) and science were at one on this point: this can no longer go on. The world has become neutral.

Yet, I remain stuck with the problem of Lovell and his edifying story and with Augustine who saw the divine light. Do the factual internal and external worlds still have a voice? Can we still try to listen to that voice *more or less* as the young Indians tried to understand the owls? Has our consciousness changed or hasn't it? Was Augustine's experience of God not still archaic, even though he found the light above and not inside the world, on "the other side" and not on "this side"? Let us keep closer to our own time and ask how Lovell could read the story of creation. Perhaps there were two Lovells, one a hard-baked pioneer who had to rely on his "coolness" and his instruments, and the other a nice Methodist who also still believed in a God. It would not be the first time that people do contradictory things and keep on living with conflicts in their private philosophy, and therefore with "cognitive dissonances" (Festinger). The archaic element in us does not die, and it arises again in our consciousness in moments when we are helpless: a dream, a cold, childishness or suspended somewhere between the moon and the earth: "the silence of infinite space frightens me" (*le silence des espaces infinis m'effraie*). It is probable that the American explorer was no less sensitive than Pascal.

Perhaps, however, we should say that there was *no dissonance*. Is there some intolerable "dissonance" when a scientist comes home in the evening, forgets his formulas and microscopes, and reaches for an anthology of poetry? Our knowledge proceeds on more than one line. The poet sees the world in a wholly different light from that of the explorer. Does this make his truth less valid? The poet has no more difficulty in understanding the language of owls than the psalmist found it difficult to understand the language of celestial bodies, which touched him right across the vastness of space. The understanding, the cognitive function of the believer, ancient man, the child and the poet have in common that they all ask different questions about the world, and that they refuse to consider the "neutral facts" as the only reality. Even primitive man already lived in two worlds, that of the gods and that of primitive technology. He listens to the secret of things and at the same time he goes on building his canoe with subtle technological expertise. Things are both themselves and transparent, pointing to something else.

Archaic man found the numinous *in* things, and the believer of today has learned to see the divinity "above", but their symbolic function does not differ that much. Science (or the mentality which sprang from it) today occupies a large part of the believer's day, and so he finds it a little more difficult to change over to poetry and belief. But even the experience of the divine is still open to him. Some researchers (Vergote, for instance) show that today's intellectuals mistrust religious experience and hardly know it.[1] They rightly shy away from self-deception. But it is possible to have a faith which has the qualities of experience. It may perhaps be compared with the love between a husband and wife which has grown throughout the years. This love does not exactly "bowl them over", and they may laugh at the sentimental songs on the radio. Yet, they cannot do without each other. There is a lasting personal relationship with an undeniable quality of reality. Such a well-tested communion has had a long

[1] The results can best be gathered from A. Vergote, *Psychologie religieuse* (Brussels, 1966), and "Le Regard du psychologue sur le symbolisme liturgique," in *La Maison Dieu* 91 (1967); see also H. Fortmann, *Als ziende de Onzienlijke –3B Geloof en Geestelijke Gezondheid* (Hilversum, 1968), pp. 138-49 and 168-72.

pre-history, and occasionally they will have had to do something quite definite about it: they had at least to take note of each other with some constancy. It is probably in this direction that we shall have to look for the basis of a faith that has the quality of experience. Perhaps the archaic element is the "eternal human" element, on condition that we look carefully for it.

George Every/*Kelham, England*

Sacralization and Secularization in East and West in the First Millennium after Christ

The theme assigned to me is vast, and I had better begin by declaring my concern. I regard secularization and sacralization as aspects of any radical change of religion. Where one religion, or a form of the same religion, supersedes another, or infiltrates into an area where another is dominant, the value of traditional religious practice is called in question. This kind of secularization was at work in the Hellenistic world and in the Roman Empire, as it is everywhere today. It interacts with another that arises directly from the Jewish and Christian attitude to idolatry, preserved and even intensified in Islam. As traditional religious custom in Asia and Africa is eroded by the acids of urbanization and challenged by the missions, so later Greek religion was eroded by urban civilization and assailed by the Church.

Meals

A parallel might be drawn between the modern movement of labor from impoverished villages into the slums of cities, and the dispersion of slaves and freedmen in ancient times. Some of these were no doubt brought up as slaves in the larger house-

27

holds. More had been sold into slavery by poor peasant families within and beyond the frontier of the civilized world of the Roman Empire. They had lost their homes and families and their ancestral religions, but they had never become members of another family or city. They were displaced persons, ready for any underground movement, and secularized in this sense: they had no sense of loyalty to any tutelary deity, though they feared many. It would therefore be a mistake to ascribe the decline in traditional pieties to the direct influence of Christians and Jews, as it was a mistake in the last century to explain the alienation of the masses from Christianity by the influence of secularists in working-men's clubs, or of Communists. The mistake was made; an interesting instance is in Pliny's famous letter to Trajan. It would seem unlikely that the decline in the supply of sacrificial victims for Bithynian temples was precisely in proportion to the number of Christian converts at so early a date. The clue is in the sentence where it is said that "the flesh of sacrificial victims is on sale everywhere, though until recently scarcely anyone could be found to buy it". A small number of persons with conscientious objections to eating sacrificial meat might be sufficient to encourage a new type of butcher's shop. In some places, no doubt, kosher shops would benefit, but then the blame would fall on the Jews, who would be the more unwilling to sell kosher meat to Christians.

Normally, in Greek and Oriental society, as in many parts of the world still, the eating of butcher's meat was a sacrificial occasion, requiring a ritual blessing. From this very normal Gentile standpoint kosher killing was sacrifice of a sort, as the blood is ritually poured out. The same would apply to the killing of animals for meat among Muslims according to ritual prescriptions. Some Christians interpreted the rules in Acts 15, 29 as committing them to kosher. Others were shockingly singular in eating a meat dinner without any more significant ritual than a grace. But as this singular custom was probably cheaper, it spread, unless impeded by an official campaign such as Pliny's, among those who without being Christians had no sufficient attachment to the gods to make them anxious for their presence or eager to do them homage.[1]

The Christians themselves could balance the secularization of dinner with a sacralization of breaking their fast. In the increasing number of Christian families in the 2nd and 3rd centuries the weekly gathering of the local church for the celebration of the eucharist was less significant than communion day by day from the reserved elements hidden at home, probably in the bedroom. Many churches had no place of meeting where all could attend. In those which had, the absent were not necessarily sick; they might be engaged in business that could not be anticipated or postponed—for instance, they might be slaves in a household. The place of communion at home in the life of the Church is a clue to much—for instance, to the original context of infant baptism, for unbaptized children could not receive communion, nor could the little ones be conveniently left out of this domestic rite. But what may seem to us an informal, almost casual kind of sacramental practice was compatible not only with belief in the real presence but with extravagant notions of its physical effects. Hippolytus thought that no one "if he receive in faith can be hurt, even if some poison should be given to him",[2] and St. Cyprian tells of a baby who had tasted of a sacrifice: "In her violated mouth and body the eucharist could not stay; the drink sanctified in the Lord's blood erupted . . . so great is the Lord's power and majesty." [3]

This kind of sacralization was extended by association beyond the sacraments. Hippolytus tells Christians to wash their hands and pray at midnight and before they go to work. "When you

---

[1] Arnold Ehrhardt, in *The Framework of the New Testament Stories* (Manchester, 1964), pp. 276-85, held that all Christians were bound to kosher, but his interpretation of Pliny, ep. xcvi, points to the growth of a secular meat trade. He brings evidence from legal texts of the anxiety of the government to control this, in fear of a "black market".

[2] B. Botte (ed.), *La Tradition Apostolique de Saint Hippolyte* (Münster, 1963), pp. 82-83.

[3] *De lapsis*, c. 25.

sign yourself from the spittle from your mouth, you are pure right down to your feet; for this is the gift of the Holy Spirit, drops of baptismal water from the fountain in the heart of the believer." [4] Distinctions had to be preserved between the eucharistic bread and bread that was blessed for the love feast, and between this and the exorcised bread that was given to catechumens.[5] Such distinctions no doubt applied not only to such meals as were spread for the widows with the authority of the bishop, but to the domestic table. This sacralization of common life persists in the icon shrines that have replaced the box for the blessed sacrament in the Eastern Christian bedroom, and, in their Western equivalents, the crucifix or the holy picture with a kneeling desk in front of it, as well as in grace before meals and the sign of the cross in a crisis.

Places

Another kind of sacralization belongs to Christian holy places. We see a glimpse of a Christian synagogue in the Epistle of St. James.[6] By the end of the 1st century it is reasonable to suppose that such buildings were not altogether uncommon in the villages of Syria, Cilicia and Lycaonia. Resemblances between Jewish synagogues and early Christian churches, of which there are a number of early remains, point to the establishment of a standard pattern at some time in the 2nd or 3rd centuries. The common features in this include two holy places: an ark for the sacred books, commonly hidden by a veil, and the holy space, often in an apse, which in the synagogues marked the direction of the temple at Jerusalem. This was originally empty, like the Holy of Holies of the second temple, but in time it came to contain the ark with its holy load of sacred books. In Christian churches it became the place for the holy table where the eucharist was celebrated, but it was set in the direction not of the

[4] B. Botte, *op. cit.*, pp. 94-95.
[5] *Ibid.*, pp. 67-69, 72-73.
[6] Jas. 2, 1-5.

earthly Jerusalem but of the rising sun, and so of the coming of the Son of Man.[7]

Passages in the Syrian *Didascalia Apostolorum* suggest that somewhere in Syria, at some time during the 3rd century, some churches were making a much closer approximation to Jewish law and custom. In the view of the compiler of the *Didascalia* they took the ceremonial provisions of the law of Moses far too seriously. I would suggest that this is a probable context for the introduction into Christian worship of such ideas of ritual purity as appear in later prohibitions against communion after sexual intercourse or during a woman's periods.[8] The sources of these need not be Jewish; they could have arisen from the assimilation of Christian shrines to pagan country shrines. The gifts that were brought to Christian presbyters and bishops in the church, and taken to the holy place, must necessarily look like sacrifices. The ritual prayers prescribed for their acceptance in manuals like that of Hippolytus [9] had a considerable currency in the East, but as they gave color to this confusion further provisions had to be laid down against the offering of such gifts actually in the church and with the eucharist.[10]

Times

Hippolytus himself, in recommending prayer at midnight, speaks of it as the hour at which nature stops and starts.[11] He already had some sense of participation in the rhythm of night and day. We know from the inscription on his memorial that the paschal cycle was one of his preoccupations. It follows that he shared the objections made by many Christians to the Jewish

---

[7] Mt. 24, 27; *Didascalia Apostolorum*, c. xii, ed. C. Connolly (Oxford, 1929), pp. 119-20; N. Boulet, "L'autel dans l'antiquité chretienne," in *Maison-Deiu* 29 (1952), pp. 45-48; L. Bouyer, "Jewish and Christian Liturgies," in *True Worship*, ed. L. Sheppard (Baltimore and London, 1963).

[8] In the replies of the Patriarch Timothy of Alexandria (381-90). Comments by Byzantine canonists are in *Pat. Graec.* 138, c. 893-4.

[9] B. Botte, *op. cit.*, pp. 18-19, 74-79.

[10] In the *Apostolic Canons* 2-4.

[11] B. Botte, *op. cit.*, pp. 94-95; cf. *I Clement*, c. 24.

way of calculating the passover. One of these was that the Jews might sometimes keep the passover before the new year began at the spring equinox. The implication of this objection [12] is that the Christian pasch is more than the commemoration of the death and resurrection of Christ, that it is in some sense a spring feast and an annual celebration of the first creation. Genesis 1 was and still is among the prophecies.

The place of the calendar in the Christian life increased as Christian shrines replaced others as the effective religious centers of towns and villages. This may be seen in the growth of another cycle around another feast besides the pasch and Pentecost—the Epiphany. In some places this was the time of the blessing of cisterns to hold the winter rains. In these areas it became a time for baptisms, and so for the celebration of the baptism of Christ. In some places it was regarded as his birthday, and later, as another birthday of Christ came in from the West, connected with his manifestation to the wise men. Advent probably [13] began as preparation for baptism at the Epiphany, as Lent began with preparation for the paschal baptisms. Both had links with the agricultural year—Lent with the time of scarcity before any new crops came, Epiphany with the winter rain. An inscription at Laodicea in Lycaonia,[14] at any rate, suggests the presence there, before Diocletian's last great persecution, of a church plant, including "stoai and tetrastoai and paintings and screens and a water tank and entrance gateway". "Even the water tank," says Sir William Ramsay,[15] "was intended not as a baptistery for hieratic purposes, but simply to provide a supply of water for public convenience; this is proved by the cisterns of many establishments, similar in character but smaller in scale . . . found elsewhere in Lycaonia. . . . At Laodicea, under the hills, the tank held running water."

[12] *Ap. Const.* V, c. 17; *Ap. Canon* 7; Socrates, *Hist. Ecc.* i, c. 9; Sozomen, *Hist. Ecc.* vii, c. 18.
[13] Traces of a long advent remain in the Armenian calendar.
[14] *Expositor* (series vii) 6 (1908), pp. 387-88.
[15] W. Ramsay, *Luke the Physician* (London, 1908), p. 154.

If the tank were an addition, as it may have been, when the church was rebuilt under Constantine, it is still clear that in many places the link between the Church's year and the natural rhythm of the seasons is older than the Christian empire. In re-regard to the pasch, it is impossible to build up an absolute anti-thesis between the spring feast and the commemoration of the historical death of Christ. In the case of Christmas and Epiphany the idea of the birth of the year is probably primary, and yet one or both of these feasts must be older than the 4th century.

Classes

There were other forms of sacralization that developed with the growth of a clerical class from the 2nd to the 5th century. All that I would emphasize at this point is an important differ-ence between East and West—namely that in parts of the East the Christian clergy were guardians of shrines as well as of sacraments before they were otherwise privileged. In the Latin West some similar developments took place in north Africa, but often in shrines of martyrs not recognized by the Church at large. In western Europe generally, the Christian clergy emerged as a class with social significance outside their own small communities in consequence of the exemptions granted to them in and after 312 by Constantine and later Christian emperors. These were not generally extended to the East until Constantine's victory over Licinius in 323, and the effect there was rather different.

In many Eastern cities, the Christian bishops and deacons al-ready had an assured position. They had nothing to gain, and probably something to lose, by making too much of privileges given to them by an unpopular and vexatious government. Therefore the lesser officers of the Church—acolytes, gravedig-gers, doorkeepers—did not hasten to enroll themselves among the clergy, and these functions never became "minor orders". Like readers and singers, and indeed most presbyters, many dea-cons, and some bishops, they continued in their ordinary occupa-tions as they had done before. The difference between clerics and others in the East lay in the strictness with which they were excluded from occupations previously banned for all Christians.[16] By imperial dispensation readers and singers, and sometimes even subdeacons or deacons, might hold posts in the civil service, but stricter canonists disapproved, and their objections were maintained by strong supporters of protocol and precedent in the service, like the Emperor Constantine Porphyrogenitus who, in the case of a retired singer investing his savings in a sinecure, regarded it as "a great disgrace . . . if a cleric becomes protospatharius".[17]

The Byzantine empire has been described with some justification as a sacred monarchy, but the clergy were not part of the governing class. The civil service had its own schools, distinct from those of the Church, and regarded with some suspicion by stricter clergy and monks. No doubt many of the children in those schools sang in church choirs, and shared in the theological enthusiasms characteristic of Byzantine congregations, where sermons were cheered and hissed and a difference in the chants sung by the choir might produce an uproar, but the masters at secular schools were not supposed to concern themselves with theology, which was the preserve of church schools and the choirs of churches and monasteries. In the lives of saints it is often implied or stated that the holy man, though skilled in secular wisdom, left it all to follow his vocation, or that the holy boy neglected secular learning and devoted himself instead to psalmody, prayer and the love of God. No doubt those civil servants who became monks and bishops in middle age brought to the Church not only administrative experience but intellectual gifts that would be applied to the ordering of theological ideas, but they were generally regarded with some suspicion by the more austere ascetics. To the Eastern Christian mind, what made a theologian was not so much learning as an experience in

---

[16] Interpretations of these rules by Byzantine canonists are in *Patr. Graec.* 138, c. 70-96.

[17] *De administrando imperio*, c. 50, ed. G. Moravcsik (Budapest, 1949), p. 245.

prayer that could be used for spiritual direction. The learning of the schools was distrusted in the monasteries. The Byzantine civil service, like all bureaucracies, was a conservative force, but Byzantine monasticism provided a nucleus of resistance to pressure from the government.

This became evident very early in the history of the Christian empire and Christian monasticism. The great cities of the East, especially Alexandria, Antioch and Constantinople, were very difficult to control. At Alexandria in particular, where the patriarch was archbishop of the whole of Egypt and commanded the fervent loyalty of the solitaries of the desert as well as of the communities organized by Pachomius, a clash between the patriarch and the prefect could make government impossible. To dispatch the patriarch into prison or exile could only add to the prefect's difficulties. The worst situation of all could develop if the patriarch lurked in the desert and sent messages of encouragement to his partisans in the back streets. Alexandria was especially hard to control, and there the Byzantine government in the end failed altogether, but at Constantinople too, at the beginning of the 5th century, St. John Chrysostom went into exile from the house guarded by his friends, leaving the cathedral and the senate house in flames. This was at the end of a whole series of disturbances arising out of his preaching, in the course of which he had been deposed by a synod and restored by the clamor of his supporters. This has a bearing on the idea of the sacred because it underlines the danger to public order involved in regard for inspired fervor. One safeguard against this was the secularity of the public service, whose members were at any rate supposed not to be passionate partisans. Interference by the government in the affairs of the Church was often unfortunate, but nearly always on the side of moderation. The iconoclast emperors, who did support an extreme faction, were also supporters of the army against the bureaucracy.

In the West there were no such safeguards. The public service was indeed secularized as support was withdrawn from traditional rites, not only by the government, but by city councils, who must often have met demands for arrears of taxation by selling the temple treasures, and then the lead off the roof, instead of their own plate, but the result of this was to undermine the dwindling prestige of the cities themselves. In Gaul and Spain many disappeared, and where city life had deeper roots, as in Italy, the ruined aristocracies had to share their powers with the bishop and his clergy, who were exempt from their special burdens, and gained influence in an impoverished world through their administration of charities. Those who thought that the empire was being ruined by the offense given to the traditional gods had a case strong enough, at any rate on the surface, to challenge all the controversial energies of St. Ambrose and St. Augustine. The plain fact is that the triumph of the Church accompanied the complete collapse of orderly government. What remained of civilization—in the sense of education in a body of knowledge, including law and letters—could only be preserved by being sacralized. The rise of the temporal power of the pope is only an outstanding instance—better documented than others for a number of reasons—of what happened in most Italian cities in the 6th and 7th centuries.

As the State collapsed, the Church gradually undertook those functions of government which require for their operation an educated class. Even when these were done in the name of the king or the emperor, they were done by clerics who, by definition, were primarily members of the clergy. Because education became their monopoly, its tools were so far sacralized that the pagan classics, including mathematical and astrological textbooks, were treated as sacred books open to mystical interpretation. In the West, objects, times and places were holy because they were ordained and guarded by a holy class with mysterious learning, assimilated in the popular mind to the bards who preserved traditional lore by Welsh and Irish firesides in the manner of Druids, Brahmins and Siberian Shamans. Their strange haircut, the tonsure, marked their special sacred character. Its precise cut became a matter of controversy between those who came from Rome, the center of civilization, and those who derived their learning from Irish monasteries, but in the outcome the tonsure became the sign of entry not only into a monastery, but into the larger class of the lettered, whose leaders were celibate (at any rate in theory), though the rank and file were married clerks (and some of these might attain positions reserved for celibates if these were not available).

In the East there was no such class. There were monks who belonged to holy mountains and similar holy places, and clergy who belonged to churches. The men of learning were different, and open to criticism from the monks, as monks were open to criticism from men of learning. In this way the "sacred palace" of the Byzantine emperor preserved a distinction between sacred and secular. Further east, under Muslim rule, this distinction was unmistakable, for, in the lands ruled by the caliph and his emirs, the civil servants might be Christians (of several confessions), Jews or Muslims. The learning necessary to produce an administrator or a physician was carefully guarded from any denominational affiliation. It is in the West that the sacred is confused with the civilized, and so secularized into a benefice, a piece of family property, or a qualification in the liberal arts.

At the end of the first millennium, all the Western churches, including Rome, were in danger of becoming family shrines, where rites were performed by clerks who might be members or servants of the family, under the direction of a lay lord or his lady. Monks continued to protest, in the West as in the East, against this and other forms of secularization of the sacred, but in Western monasticism the sacralization of power was taken for granted. Some of the monasteries on Mount Athos came to possess estates elsewhere, but their political power was limited to their mountain sanctuary. The order of Cluny became a power everywhere, largely because well-ordered monastic communities were havens of peace that grew rich on the labors of refugees. But the sacralization of power is always dangerous. Some distinction between sacred and secular is vital to any religion. That in Christ the common has become holy and the holy has become common does not make them one and the same, for his kingdom is not of this world, and to sacralize civilization is to anticipate the millennium.

Michel Meslin/*Paris, France*

Ecclesiastical Institutions and Clericalization from 100 to 500 A.D.

From the beginning the Christian Church was in a peculiar situation. It was a community of faithful with a monotheistic religion surrounded by many forms of polytheism, soon severed from the Jews among whom it originated and who had been granted freedom of worship by Rome. How could it realize its evangelizing mission, its ecumenical vocation, while presenting itself, as Adolf Harnack rightly put it, as "a religion of high morality, of sanctity and of the Spirit"? How did this new religion spread and how far could it penetrate its pagan environment when it seemed separated from this society in everything?

This Christian Church was also a society. The word "Church" appears in all the patristic writings and has, according to the context, a meaning strictly connected with worship—a gathering of faithful for worship—or a sociological meaning—a local community gathered round a bishop (the Church of Rome, the Church of Antioch, etc.). But whether as a whole or in part, the Church has always seen itself as a society of faithful, of those who believe in Christ, share in the same sacramental life and live in the same hope. Like all other societies, the Christian Church pursued a specific aim and had, by sheer internal necessity, to develop hierarchical institutions, while the unfolding of the revealed message led to a theology which was above all a normative science. This theology naturally inspired an ethic which put the Christians in a dialectical relationship of both opposition to and participation in their pagan surroundings. The structures of the ecclesiastical organization developed only very gradually, while at the same time the essential dogmas were formulated. Thus there was a parallel development of the elaboration of the scriptural canon, the creeds and a hierarchical ministry, and these three developments were legitimized in a tradition of the Church by reference to a common apostolic origin. The question therefore arises whether the development of ecclesiastical institutions during the early centuries could have led partly not only to a certain isolation of the Christians in a still pagan society but even to an isolation of the clergy from the mass of the faithful. This question became more pressing still when their peculiar situation in an occasionally hostile State underwent a profound modification in the 4th century. First recognized, then "established" in an empire that had become Christian, the Church became more institutionalized and developed a certain clericalization, a process which we can try to outline in detail.[1]

I

Immediately after Pentecost the apostles proceeded, first in Jerusalem, then in the churches founded by St. Paul, to install a clergy who constituted, under their guidance, an intermediate body between God and the rest of the Christians (Acts 6, 1-7; 15, 2. 4. 6; 20, 17). As far as the vagueness of the terms allows,

[1] For further reading on the subject matter of this article, cf. A. Harnack, *Die Mission und Ausbreitung des Christentums* (Leipzig, 1902); J. Colson, *L'Evêque dans les communautés primitives* (Paris, 1951); J. Gaudemet, *L'Eglise dans l'Empire romain* (Paris, 1959); J. von Campenhausen, *Kirchliches Amt und geistliche Vollmacht in den ersten drei Jahrhunderten* (Tübingen, 1963); R. Hernegger, *Religion, Frömmigkeit, Kult* (Weilheim, 1961); A. Hamman, *Vie liturgique et vie sociale* (Paris, 1968). See also G. Every's article in this volume.

we see that the presbyters/*episcopi* are entrusted with a power to teach and with the preservation of the deposit of faith while the deacons combine a liturgical function with the social service of the community, under the strict authority of the bishop. This hierarchical structure of every Christian community is never a power delegated by the community but draws its authority directly from Christ via the apostles who first instituted it. According to the Lord's own words, the bishop has the power of the keys to govern the society of Christians, the Church (Jn. 21, 15; Mt. 28, 19; Mk. 16, 15). This hierarchical structure is already prominent at the end of the 1st century in the Epistle of Clement of Rome where the organization of the Roman legion is put forward as a model (XXXVII), and where he lays down as an absolute rule that there must be a "subordination according to the charisma with which each has been endowed" (XXXVIII, 1).

At about the same time Ignatius of Antioch developed a theological interpretation of such a hierarchical organization: every church is united to a single bishop who represents Christ and is the visible center of that unity in love, so that, surrounded by the presbyters and deacons, the bishop appears as the incarnation of the community over which he presides. The faithful owe obedience to this college of presbyters who govern with the bishop and share in his powers, as they owe it to the apostles of Jesus Christ (*Trall.* II, 2; III; XIII; *Magn.* II; VI; VII; *Smyrn.* VIII; *Eph.* II; XX; etc.) because "the bishop is the image of the Father and the presbyters are the senate of God, the college of apostles" (*Trall.* III, 1). For Irenaeus of Lyons, the most important of the 2nd-century theologians, the bishop embodies, in every community and every generation of Christians, the Church's tradition derived from the apostles, and he is both the heir and guarantee of this tradition. Thus sacralized, the hierarchical authority in the Church inspires and directs the life of all the Christian communities. Cyprian of Carthage (d. 258) went a step further. In the interpreter of the community of the faithful, God's choice becomes manifest and irrevocable and endows the elected bishop with a special charisma: "God's majesty ordains him to the service of the Church. . . . God's power and goodness protect him in his function . . . for the Lord who deigns to choose and establish his pontiffs protects with his will and aids with his assistance those he has thus chosen and established" (*Ep.* LV, 9, 2; XLVIII, 4, 2). Thus the bishop's power assumes monarchical features and has become sacralized to such a point that the function of Christians as a whole in the election of a bishop loses its efficacy throughout the early period.

It is true that the *Apostolic Tradition* of Hippolytus of Rome still declared that "he must be ordained bishop who has been chosen by the people" and that Cyprian also said "that the community has the power to choose its bishop or to reject one imposed by force" (*Ep.* LXVII, this occurs in the context of a local controversy), but in practice this voting right of the people was more and more restricted. The people, gathered in the metropolitan church, acclaimed a name proposed by the neighboring bishops and the presbyterium. Although this popular participation was still an historical fact in the 3rd and 4th centuries (cf. the election of Ambrose, Martin, and others), its real importance continued to decrease. When Pope Celestine wrote in 429 to the bishops of Calabria and Apulia, he advised that, in case of an episcopal election, "the people must be taught, not followed" (*Ep.* V, 3). One should add that by the 5th century this Christian "people" had come to comprise only the "notables" of the city: the election had become a matter of local negotiations in which the voice of the metropolitan and the neighboring bishops was decisive (Can. 4, 6, of Nicea). Popular joy vented itself in a collective acclamation and so endorsed a decision in which the faithful had had no part whatever.

The function of the deacon went through a similar course of clericalization during the first four centuries of our era. Up until about the second half of the 3rd century, the deacon's function was essentially one of charitable and social activity within the community. Closely linked with the bishop, the deacon was the minister of charity and of service, carrying out the *diakonia* of Christ just as the bishop was the visible witness of love in the unity of his Church. The deacon, ordained for "the service of the tables" rather than for preaching and performing in the liturgy, busied himself with the concrete affairs of the community, such as the finances and the "meals of charity" or *agapes*. But as the priestly function developed toward the end of the 3rd century, the function of the deacon changed. While the priesthood developed its own sphere of action, the deacon saw his function more and more reduced to playing a part on the fringe of the liturgy. Still closely dependent on the bishop, but now also on the priest, the diaconate tended to become a kind of way of assisting the priest or, at least, a transitional phase in the ecclesiastical order, the "cursus", clear evidence of the clericalization which absorbed the development of the ecclesiastical structures.

Something similar happened in the financial organization of the community. The *koinonia,* the sharing of personal wealth among Christians, the organization of which was one of the principal functions of the deacon, had proved a failure, with the result that the offerings of the faithful were seen as something inherent in the fact of having personal wealth. By a curious return to old Israelitic custom, these offerings were then interpreted as an obligatory institution, the tithe, which affected the whole Christian people and was then assigned to the provision of the needs of the clergy, and soon enough those Christians who would refuse to cooperate in this were anathematized (*Apost. Const.* VIII, 29, 2; 4th Roman Synod under Damasus, *Mansi* III, p. 642; Augustine, *Enarr. in Ps.* 103, 1; *Tract. in Jo.* 122, 3; Jerome, *Ep.* LII, 5). In his *Opus imperfectum in Mattaeum* (*PG* 56, p. 884), Bishop Maximinus goes so far as to specify that the quantity of the tithe to be collected must correspond to the hierarchical function of the recipient. Thus, from the middle of the 3rd century, we observe the development of a clericalizing process which assumed constantly wider proportions after the Christian Church had been recognized by the Roman Empire.

II

While in each church a bi-polar structure developed of clergy and laity, as had already happened at Carthage since Cyprian, a hierarchy of various ranks developed within the clerical sphere. The specific place of each clerical group was carefully defined by a religious legal system, and the succession of the various functions, disturbed over major and minor orders, was organized in a regular sequence, a *cursus*. When the Roman State gave the Christian Church privilege of place, it was natural that civil law would spell out a veritable statute for the clergy who, by the same token, became a separate class of citizens. Because they were consecrated to the service of God, the clergy were given special privileges which raised them to a specific kind of dignity in the closed State and society of the later empire. Before 472 they enjoyed in fact, and since then also by right, a patrimonial statute which allowed them to dispose freely of their personal goods and that without the legal obligations linked to the position of the father of a family (*Cod. Just.* I, 3, 33); if they died intestate and without heirs, their goods returned to their church (*Cod. Th.* V, 3, 1, of 434). But it was above all the various fiscal exemptions (no land tax and no *capitatio plebeia*) as well as the exemption from civic and municipal functions (*Cod. Th.* XVI, 2, 2, of 313; XVI, 2, 7, of 330), which constituted the most coveted privilege at a time when harsh taxation weighed heavily upon every citizen of the empire so that municipal functions and civic duties were shied away from or left untended. Lastly, this statute of the clergy was rounded off by the privilege of a separate jurisdiction. It appeared that since the clergy judged in the name of God, they could not themselves be judged by ordinary civil courts but only by their bishops or their peers. This was the prerogative of a constituted body and not a favor granted to individuals, and so this privilege of a separate clerical jurisdiction (*privilegium fori*) recognized the total autonomy of the clerical society and its hierarchy right in the middle of the Roman Empire (*Cod. Th.* XVI, 2, 12 of 412, which makes a vague attempt at trying to limit its application).

But it is not only their preferential civil statute which made the clergy of the "Constantinian" Church look different from all other citizens of the empire, Christian or not. In his *De officiis,* St. Ambrose of Milan tried to rewrite a treatise by Cicero as a veritable textbook of clerical morality by mixing Cicero's stoic ideals with Christian morality. Although the clergy are not yet dressed differently, the tonsure appeared after 360 in the East and in the second half of the 5th century in Rome. The requirement to lead an ascetic life and the obligation of celibacy from the lectorate upward (Council of Carthage, c. 19, of 397; Leo the Great, Ep. XVI, 4, etc.) or of marital continence when they were already married (Council of Elvira, c. 33; of Carthage, c. 2, in 390), separated the clergy from the ordinary faithful, while the influence of monachism led to greater insistence on poverty and a communal life, sometimes organized around the bishop (Jerome, *Ep. ad Nepotianum*).

But with the indelible effect of their ordination the clergy have above all the prerogative of the "power of order" (*potestas ordinis*): they alone can administer the sacraments, the eucharist, penance and baptism (except in the specific case of danger of death, and even in this case the exception was not often made use of), and if in some Eastern Churches deaconesses performed certain baptismal rites for women who must not be exposed to the eyes of men, clergy or not, the reason was that these deaconesses belonged to the local clergy. While in the apostolic age charismatic helpers shared in the Church's teaching function, this function was increasingly reserved to the bishop alone. Occasionally the spread of Christianity made it necessary to let simple priests share in the preaching. This, however, was far from general practice. In 431 in his letter to the bishops of Gaul, Pope Celestine feared that if priests were allowed to preach they might make doctrinal errors (*Ep.* XXI, 2). In spite of all this, however, certain exceptions were bound to creep in. Thus the *Apostolic Constitutions* give one to understand that the simple faithful could preach if they were both good Christians and good speakers. But this use of the laity could only occur in mission countries—Ireland, for instance, and even then rarely; where Christianity had long been established, as in Rome, Alexandria or Carthage, the teaching of the faith was strictly reserved to the bishop who could on occasion delegate certain clerics to do it (Leo the Great, *Ep.* CXIX, 6 and CXX, 6).

Not only in the administration of the sacraments and preaching were the clergy set apart from the laity, but even in the sanctuary. The part of the church where the sacrifice was celebrated was out of bounds to the faithful who were separated from the altar by curtains or barriers which marked off the chancel (Council of Laodicea, c. 4, of 365). When Emperor Theodosius tried to occupy a seat near the altar, Ambrose sent him back to the nave with the other faithful. Thus the very organization of the places of worship underlined the eminence of the clergy as being reserved to the service of God. In numbers, however, this clerical world remained very small. Although texts are sporadic and the documentation is full of lacunae, it is possible here and there to assess the extent of this clerical society. In the middle of the 3rd century, Rome counted 112 clergy at various levels of the hierarchy (Eusebius of Caesarea, *Eccl. Hist.* VI, 43, 11), and in the 5th century about 300. Under the reign of the Vandals, Carthage is said to have had about 500 clergy (Victor de Vita, *Hist. pers.* III, 34). But these were the two capital cities of the West. In Sirmium, even though it was an imperial residence, the clerical community counted only some ten members in 366 (*Altercatio Heracliani;* Hilary of Poitiers, *Fr. Hist.* V).

III

Whatever the local situation, it is clear that in each church there co-existed "two kinds of Christians" *(duo genera Chris-*

tianorum). The expression occurs in Gratian (*Decr.,* C 12, qu.
1, c. 7), who says that in using these words he was inspired by
St. Jerome (*Letter to Nepot.*). How, then, can we reconcile the
existence of a hierarchy, claiming to be founded by the apostles
and to have the power of the keys, with the existence of a
brotherhood made up of the children of God? How can we sublimate the opposition between a clerical order (*ordo*) and a *plebs*
of ordinary faithful in a right understanding of the Church as the
body of Christ? With Lactantius, Victorinus of Pettau and Jerome, Augustine in his *City of God* explains the words of the
Apocalypse "they will be priests" as follows: "These words must
not be understood as applying only to bishops and priests—that
is, the clerical body—but to all Christians who are all called
priests and members of the one high priest in virtue of their
mystical anointment" (XX, 10).

What room was there left in the life of the Church for that
"chosen race, that royal priesthood, that consecrated nation" of
which St. Peter speaks (1 Pet. 2, 9)? The whole doctrinal history of the 4th and 5th centuries shows how much the Arian and
christological conflicts excited public opinion and stirred up collective passions and attitudes in a way which surprises us. Arius
was the first to think of spreading his theology by means of
popular ditties which seamen, longshoremen and travelers hum-
med in the port of Alexandria. In the public baths or at the
baker's, people seriously debated the question whether the
Father was greater than the Son. Thus in the East, more than
in the West, except in Milan at the time of St. Ambrose, the laity
brought to bear their congenital taste for theological discussion
of complex doctrinal problems. In the great Eastern cities, such
a philosophical controversy provoked an agitation which frequently led to political and popular riots (Alexandria, Constantinople, Antioch), and this was also true even in the West (Rome
and Milan). But this never implied an effective, constant and
juridical participation of the Christian laity in ecumenical synods or provincial synods. The definition and preservation of
the faith remained the prerogative of the clergy. With the ex-

ception of certain important imperial officials who represented
the State of Rome in those ecclesiastical gatherings by order, the
few faithful who were present at provincial synods were there
only as observers or witnesses, and they signified their consent
by answering "Amen" when the canons were solemnly promul-
gated at the end.

This need not raise any eyebrows. In actual fact, when the
Church settled down somewhat triumphantly in the empire, no
one could possibly identify the faithful as a whole with that
"people of saints", that "chosen race" of the days of the apostles.
At the beginning of the 4th century, Eusebius of Caesarea was
already aware of this, and he clearly distinguished two categories of Christians, those, the vast majority, who lived in the
world and tried to observe the rules of faith and morals of
the Church as well as they could, and those who, "moved only by
the love of heavenly things, can fulfill the function of inter-
cessors" (*Demonstr. evang.* I, 8). Hence the distinction, even
among the laity themselves, of an elite, also "hierarchical", com-
prising monks, virgins, widows and all those who detached themselves from the mass of the faithful by the practice of self-denial,
chastity, poverty and commitment. They, too, were given a canonical legislation which spelled out their rights and duties. Widowhood thus became an "order" within the laity, and widows
could make "profession" of their widowhood in a special cere-
mony before the bishop which recalls the solemn profession of
virgins (Council of Orange, c. 27, of 441; *Statuta Eccl. ant.*,
c. 104). These widows were put in charge of the preparation
for baptism (*ibid.*, c. 12) and were bound to recite the *opus
Dei*, the prayer for the community which provided them with a
livelihood (*ibid.*, c. 103).

In the same way, the statute of virgins consecrated to God,
which had remained very vague, became more detailed from the
4th century on, as the number of nuns increased: In the West,
their consecration was given a ritual; the "taking of the veil"
(*velatio*) took place at Christmas, the Epiphany or Easter, before a Christian congregation gathered around the bishop who

alone had the right to consecrate virgins (Councils of Carthage of 390 and 397), and in Gaul also gave them a special habit (*Stat. Eccl. Ant.*, c. 99). There also grew a tendency to make them live in community (Councils of Carthage of 397, c. 33, and of 419, c. 44). At the same time, their status was more or less officially recognized by the fact that civil law protected them against all violence and severely punished any attempt to interfere with their vocation (*Cod. Th.* IX, 25, 1, of 354; IX, 25, 2, of 364; IX, 25, 3, of 420, etc.).

The extraordinary development of monachism from the beginning of the 4th century shows still more clearly that for some Christians, seized with the desire for perfection, the only way possible was to flee the world. This was a substitute for a martyrdom that was no longer possible once the Church was not only recognized but even endowed with numerous privileges. Throughout the East, and then in Gaul, Italy and Africa, Christians began to form groups in order to lead an eremitical or cenobitic existence independently of each other, without adopting the priesthood, and devoting their lives to prayer and asceticism. It is not really important that in the 4th century there were not yet any clearly defined "monastic rules", or that the conditions of admission varied from one place to another (as for the Hindu *ashram* today), or that the ecclesiastical and civil statute of the monks was not formulated until later (the first council to impose the duty of obedience was that of Chalcedon). What is important is that the Church gave pride of place in the lay hierarchy to those who in one way or another had renounced the world. Often ill understood—and not only by the pagans—those monks, virgins and widows bore witness not only to the simplicity of the children of God in the midst of an often triumphalist Church but also to a certain incompatibility between the kingdom of God and the empire, even a Christian empire.

While the clergy in practice monopolized all spiritual responsibility for the Christian community and the cream of the laity withdrew from the world in order to lead a life of poverty, obedience and prayer, the secular problems remained the responsibility of the remaining Christians. First among these was the problem of a Church that had become rich but was also responsible for social assistance. It seems that, throughout the early centuries, the clergy were torn between the desire to let the layman administer the Church's property and the desire to preserve all the prerogatives of their authority. Since the Church's wealth belonged by right to each local church, the bishop alone had supreme control over the administration of that ecclesiastical patrimony, and he was totally free to handle it as he saw fit. For this he was only responsible to God (Council of Antioch of 341, cc. 24 and 25; *Canons of the Apostles,* 39; Gelasius, *Ep. XIV,* 27; XV, 2, etc.). In Africa, however, where Christians clung to old traditions, the laity had a share in the administration of the Church's wealth. They were the *seniores laici* (lay elders) who were elected by the people and managed ecclesiastical property, fixed income charges and looked after the upkeep of the buildings used for worship. But toward the end of the 4th century, ecclesiastical legislation limited lay intervention in this field. The Council of Gangres put the management of such property into the hands of treasurers who had to be clerics, and this arrangement was made obligatory by the Council of Chalcedon (c. 26). At Hippo, in the West, Augustine used a priest administrator who had to render an account each year (Possidius, *Vita Aug.* 24).

In Rome itself the properties attached to the great basilicas were administered by clerical officers (*praepositi*) accountable to the ecclesiastical authority only. On the other hand, the laity were asked to finance the new churches and support those in charge in the vast domains of the wealthy (*potentiores*). This was a dangerous and shortsighted practice since the big landowners, who built at their own expense and on ground which belonged to them, naturally came to look on such churches as an integral part of their territory, like their barns and workshops. From the end of the 4th century civil law distinguished public churches from private ones, (*Cod. Th.* XVI, 5, 14, of 388) and required that, in the latter case, the priest in charge should be taken from the people of that property. To counter this danger of lay appropriation of a property rightly or wrongly considered as belonging to the Church, the Councils of the following century constantly insisted on the authority of the bishop as solely competent to nominate a priest in charge and to administer the property of his Church (Council of Orange of 411, c. 10, etc.).

IV

This inevitable institutional development in the Church is not the only cause of the rift which gradually appeared between the clergy and the "religious" laity on the one hand, and the mass of the faithful on the other. As one observes the development of society, culture and collective attitudes in the later empire, another crack appears which demands careful analysis, taking into account the period and region under discussion.

The monks, leading their life of asceticism and perfection and detached from the material cares and habits of the other citizens of the empire, showed in their personal lives the "scandal" created by the first Christians. The demands made by their worship and moral pursuit seemed to put them apart from their society. On the other hand, the sociological progress of Christianity, which had become the majority religion in the cities, introduced Christianity to those social elements which were most impervious to its spiritual message—namely, the aristocracy, the upper middle class and the intellectuals. Via a social ascent which had already begun toward the end of the 3rd century, Christianity came to shed its cultural inferiority complex, became open to the world, and accepted without demur the wealth of traditional culture which it had both despised and feared for a long time.

It is not purely accidental that, with the well-known exception of Augustine, almost all the great theologians and bishops of the end of antiquity came from the leading social sectors of the later Roman Empire. All had studied at the imperial universities; some had served the State in one capacity or another before taking office in the Church. In fact, the patristic age is the era when for the first time a Christian humanism appeared, the original elaboration of a Christian philosophy with a specific ethic and view of the world and no longer afraid of embodying some of the values inherent in secular culture. It seems therefore obvious that the bishop of that age was much closer to his flock because of his social background and intellectual culture than would have been the case in the 2nd century. This was the more so since his episcopal duties were not limited to his religious office. Vested, since Constantine (*Cod. Th.* I, 27, 1), with judicial power in general, the bishop often had to play a part in his city which was the more burdensome as, with the spread of Christianity, numerous Christian plaintiffs preferred to go to the bishop's tribunal rather than the civil tribunal. In actual fact, the bishop's function always remained that of a conciliator rather than that of a real judge, and the imperial administrators did all they could to restrain the powers of that ecclesiastical jurisdiction which Constantine had rather too generously and imprudently granted (*Cod. Just.* II, 1, 10, of Arcadius in 398; *Cod. Th.* XVI, 11, 1).

But if in matters of society and culture the bishop and his clergy often took part in the life of their faithful, the same cannot be said with regard to the ordinary conditions of social life. The Christianization of the actual living conditions was one of the sectors where paganism, deeply rooted in the collective mentality, was most tenacious. The Church failed to give liturgical names to the days of the week and to fix the beginning of the Christian year at Christmas. In spite of persistent preaching by a large number of bishops, the use of the liturgical term *feria,* followed by an ordinal, succeeded nowhere except in Portugal in ousting the traditional pagan names for the days of the week (Tertullian, *De jejunio,* 2; Maximus of Turin; Augustine, *Enarr. in Ps. 93,* 3; Martin of Braga, etc.). Popular habit was in fact so strong that in Anglo-Saxon countries the days of the week are still called by their old Roman or Teutonic names. The same happened for the beginning of the year; in Roman society the civil year started with the calends of January according to the sidereal year divided into twelve months. In the 4th and 5th centuries the Church wanted to sublimate this civil time into a sacred, liturgical time which, based on an annual cycle of the principal events of Christ's life, would help the faithful to meditate on his teaching and follow his example. In this cycle only the feast of Christmas could mark the beginning, and not the calends of January, officially maintained by the "Christian" emperors as an occasion of joy and social harmony, accompanied by inaugural practices and social and sexual masquerades—in short, as a pagan feast. Though fiercely criticized by John Chrysostom, Asterius of Apamea, Augustine, Maximus of Turin, Martin of Braga and Isidore of Seville, the custom persisted in the countryside throughout the West up to World War I.

The Church's attempt to regulate time was wholly out of tune with popular feeling. This was not accidental. In the 5th century, Christianity had ceased being an urban phenomenon and had slowly penetrated into the rural world which had remained pagan. This process showed up a serious gap between a human nature, still close to sacred natural phenomena known and cherished for centuries, and a religious culture which was bound to be seen as imposed from outside. As the clergy became aware of the new problems thus created, the Church set up new institutions, and one can already see the beginnings of a pattern of rural parishes, established either in the *pagus,* the rural center far from the city, or on the large properties which had already developed a medieval structure.

New canonical legislation tried to eliminate this popular and rural paganism. A new pastoral strategy was developed, more adapted to the peculiar milieu of the countryside (Martin of Braga, *De catechizandis rudibus;* the sermons of Caesarius of Arles, etc.). A new world emerged out of the chaos created by the great invasions and the establishment of barbarian kingdoms. In the West, the Christian was no longer the citizen of a universal empire, image of the kingdom of God. He had to live in new political societies, economically closed, where the old culture only survived in a decreasing elite which, without an outlet in the bureaucratic structure of the empire, remained a nursery of bishops (the case of the Apollinaris family is typical). In this barbaric age which spread throughout the West, it was left to a small group of clerics to gather in the silence of the cloisters the few traces of that Christian humanism of the golden age of the Fathers of the Church which would provide the foundations of medieval thought. In the East, the fate of Church and empire remained inextricably intertwined like the wheat and the weeds of the parable. When the time for the harvest has come, only the Lord will be able to sort out the good from the bad.

Yves Congar, O.P./*Le Saulchoir, France*

The Sacralization of Western Society in the Middle Ages

When we talk about the European Middle Ages, we readily speak about a "sacral Christendom". In this article, I should like to discuss two specific points related to the long history of this "age of faith". We shall consider: (1) the role played by the Old Testament model; (2) the restraint exercised on social movements by norms and paradigms borrowed from the transcendental world.

I

SACRAL SOCIETY AND THE OLD TESTAMENT

A Christian social order took shape when the general requirements for a Christian way of life were embodied in the public aspects and structures of societal life and the temporal city. In such a process it was normal and inevitable that people would have recourse to Old Testament models; for it was the peculiar fate of the Israelite people, as a nation, to be chosen as the People of God and to incorporate the obligations of the covenant and the exclusive cult of Yahweh in their national structures. Today we know that God willed this in the economy of salvation to preserve the fidelity of his people in the midst of idolatrous nations.

55

It gave rise to a pattern of rigorous sacralization and to a pattern of legislation designed to keep the Israelites separate from other nations.

Even before a Christian social order took shape, we find references to the Old Testament. It is interesting to note the context in which such references crop up. Two types of situations may be noted here. First of all, the institutions and legal dispositions of the Old Testament were invoked by the early Fathers (during the days of persecution) to shore up respect for the order established in the Church,[1] adherence to the norms of morality imposed on the clergy [2] and obedience to properly constituted ministers in the hierarchy.[3] These references to the Old Testament helped to fix the sacerdotal and cultic vocabulary of early Christianity and to make the clergy and the clerical state a distinctive entity.

Secondly, references to the Old Testament were used to justify the use of physical force by the State against schisms and heresies. This, of course, presupposed the conversion of the political branch to Christianity. We find such justifications very early, as soon as such laws were broached.[4]

Early Examples

In their efforts to bring a Christian morality to the peoples of Europe, especially during the period that immediately followed the invasions of the 5th century, the bishops and councils readily looked for support in the laws and models of the Old Testament. We see this in Gaul, for example, in the work of Caesarius of Arles (470-542) regarding tithes and sexual morality. Refer-

---

[1] See Clement of Rome, *Cor.* XL, 5 and XLI.

[2] See the epistle of the clergy of Rome to Cyprian, invoking Ez. 34, 3: *Inter Epp. Cypr.* VIII, 1; cf. Cyprian himself, *Ep.* I, 1; LVII, 4; LXVII, 1.

[3] See St. Cyprian, *Ep.* III, 1; IV, 4; XLIII, 7; LIX, 4; LXVI, 3—with constant citation of Deut. 17, 12-13.

[4] Firmicus Maternus in 346 (*De errore profanorum religionum*, XXIX and XXX), with citations of Ex. 22, 20 and Deut. 13, 6-18; Optatus of Mileve in 366-67, in his tract against the Donatists, III, 5 (with citations of NM 25, 11; III, 7; Moses, Phineas and Elias as examples).

ences to the Old Testament increased during the 6th century. This is particularly true in Visigoth Spain and 7th-century Ireland, where Oriental precedents may have exercised some influence.[5]

In Visigoth Spain and Merovingian Gaul, liturgical rites were a primary focal point. The first known anointing of a king was that of Wamba at Toledo in 672 (anointing of the head). Later we have the anointing of Pepin the Franc (751) and of Egfrid in England (787), with Saul and David serving as the models.

At the beginning of the 8th century, the anointing of the hands was introduced into the priestly rite of ordination, which had involved simply the imposition of hands up to that time; reference was made to the Latin translation of Exodus 28, 41 and Numbers 3, 3. Even in the 6th century, churches were consecrated simply by having the eucharist celebrated there. The 8th-century Sacramentary of Angoulême, however, sets forth a sumptuous ritual borrowed from the Old Testament: aspersion (cf. Ex. 29; Lev. 8 and 16); anointings (Ex. 30, 25-28; 40, 9-10); incensing (Ex. 30, 1; 40, 24ff.).

This passion for finding the origins of Christian institutions in the Old Testament found a focal point in the conception of the priesthood itself. St. Jerome opened the door, but it was St. Isidore of Seville, one of the most influential pedagogues of the Middle Ages, who inculcated the idea that the different ranks had their type and origin in the cultic order of the Mosaic law.[6] The linkup of Old and New Testament ideas on the priesthood was never studied in any systematic or complete fashion. Most of the time, people were content to say: *"Ordo sacerdotii a vetere lege sumpsit exordium, scilicet, a filiis Aaron."* But Isi-

[5] R. Kottje, *Studien zum Einfluss des Alten Testamentes auf Recht und Liturgie des frühen Mittelalters* (from 6th to 8th century) (Bonn, 1964); J. Chydenius, *Medieval Institutions and the Old Testament* (Helsinki, 1965).

[6] *De ecclesiasticis officiis*, II, 5ff. (*PL* 83, 781ff.). The bishop = Aaron; the priests = his sons; the deacons = the Levites; the subdeacons = the "servants" of Ezra 7, 7 and 7, 24; the exorcists = the sons of Solomon's servants; the lectors = the prophets; the porters = the temple gatekeepers.

dore's texts were transmitted and quoted throughout the medieval period. There is no doubt that they greatly helped to accentuate the *cultic* character of the priesthood.

The Irish Influence

Irish references to the Old Testament were primarily of an ethical and disciplinary cast. They were numerous and highly influential. Two-thirds of the scriptural citations (c. 500) in the *Collectio canonum Hibernensis* (7th century) were taken from the Old Testament. What could be more indicative that the very title of the *Liber ex lege Moysi* (Ireland, c. 700)? [7] The drive to connect Sunday with the Sabbath gained momentum toward the end of the 6th century, backed up by a letter of Christ that supposedly fell from heaven! It was solemnly ratified, with explicit reference to the Old Testament, at the Synod of Berstead (Kent) in 695 or 696, by the *Liber ex lege Moysi* (7th century), and by the Book of Armagh (second half of the 7th century).[8]

In like manner the *Collectio Hibernensis*, the canons of Theodore for the Anglo-Saxon church, St. Pirmin, Pépin and Charlemagne based the legal obligation of tithes on the Old Testament (see footnote 17). The Irish penitentials did not introduce anything new when they followed the lead of Leviticus and treated wet dreams as an impurity; if there was consent to them, this called for penance and abstention from communion. The penitentials also required abstention from conjugal relations on certain days.

The *Liber ex lege Moysi* picks up the prescriptions of Leviticus 12 regarding a woman in childbirth. The Irish canons or penitentials, the *Canones* of Theodore of Canterbury, also set forth certain requirements regarding abstinence from food. These prescriptions, in fact, were accepted more or less on the

---

[7] See P. Fournier, "Le Liber ex lege Moysi et les tendances bibliques du Droit canonique irlandais," in *Revue Celtique* 30 (July 1909), pp. 221-34.

[8] R. Kottje, *op. cit.*, pp. 44ff.; L. L. McReavy, "The Sunday Repose from Labor: An Historical-Theological Examination of the Notion of Servile Work," in *Eph. Theol. Lovan.* 12 (1935), pp. 291-323.

continent until the Scholastics pointed out that the Mosaic law was being continued in Christianity.[9]

Irish Christianity had great religious and cultural vitality during this period. It had a decisive influence on Charlemagne and the Carolingian renaissance, through the work of Irish apostles on the continent and through the mediation of Alcuin. It has been shown that 80 percent of Alcuin's vocabulary in social and political matters comes from the Old Testament.[10] Charlemagne is seen as Josiah, the one who reforms and revivifies cultic worship. He is seen as David, the anointed of God. Alcuin calls him precisely that.

Hagiography and the monastic texts also liked to allude to Old Testament models.[11] The text of Deuteronomy 17, 14-20 was often cited as a brief portrait of what a prince should be.[12] This practice would continue,[13] and verses 8-13 would be

[9] M. Böckenhoff, *Speisesatzungen mosaischer Art im mittelalterlichen Kirchenrechtsquellen* (Münster, 1907). It would be very interesting to examine what might be called the Scholastic's recognition of the distinctiveness of the new law, and the role played by discussions with the Jews in this process.

[10] A. Chélini, "Le vocabulaire politique et social dans la Correspondence d'Alcuin," *Annales de la Faculté des Lettres d'Aix en Provence* (1959). On the influence of the Old Testament on Charlemagne and his work, see H. Lilienfein, *Die Anschauungen von Staat und Kirche im Reich der Karolinger* (Heidelberg, 1902); M. Buchner, *Einhard als Künstler* (Strasbourg, 1919), pp. 1ff., 27ff., 32ff.; L. Halphen, *A travers l'histoire du Moyen Age* (Paris, 1950), pp. 97ff.; Etienne Delaruelle, in *Bull. Littér. eccles.* (1941), pp. 26ff.; (1954), pp. 137ff., and in *Rev. Hist. Egl. de France* (1953), pp. 173, 181-89; W. Mohr, "Christlich-alttestamentliches Gedankengut in der Entwicklung des karolingischen Kaisertums," in *Judentum im Mittelalter,* edited by P. Wilpert (Berlin, 1966), pp. 482ff.

[11] See J. Leclercq, "L'Ecriture sainte dans l'hagiographie monastique du Haut Moyen-Age," in *La Bibbia nell'Alto Medioevo* (Spoleto, 1963), pp. 103-28, 295-303.

[12] See the important Council of Paris, 829 (II, 1: MGH, *Concilia* II, 649) or Jonas of Orleans (*De institutione regia,* c. 3: ed. J. Reviron, p. 139); Hincmar of Reims, *De persona regis,* 8.

[13] By John of Salisbury in 1159 (*Policraticus* IV, 4f.: ed. Webb, I, 244f.); Halinand of Froimond, c. 1200 (*De regimine principum*); by Vincent of Beauvais in the middle of the 13th century, on the behavior of Marguerite, wife of St. Louis (*De eruditione filiorum regalium*); by Gilbert of Tournai in 1259, *Eruditio regum,* written at the behest of St. Louis.

invoked in a hierocratic sense by Innocent III in his decisive
and well-known Decretal of 1202 (*Per venerabilem.*)[14] There
Innocent III enunciated a general principle that would be
fraught with consequences: Since "Deuteronomy" means the
"second law", it indicates to us what should be observed under
the New Testament dispensation. The Reformationists would
say later that this amounted to putting the Gospel under the
law, but this accusation is unfair and excessive. However, the
fact remains that in the eyes of Innocent III the *populus Chris-
tianus,* of which he was the head (as well as being the head
of the *ecclesia*), was to some extent equated with the
populus Dei of the Old Testament.[15] This *populus* lived their
lives under a regime of sacred law which, from the time of
St. Gregory VII, tended to become hierocratic.

Carolingian Practice

In the Carolingian era, this sacral character was ensured by
the ruler and the priests together. During his lifetime, Charlemagne himself exerted much initiative in this area. After his
death, we find more and more successful involvement by the
bishops and the papacy itself. Charlemagne put great stress on
the cultic laws: abstention from servile work on Sunday,[16]
tithes,[17] liturgical rules, etc. He wanted to transform his people
into the *populus Dei.*

This program presupposed and imposed a clear measure of
conservatism and paternalism within society. The introduction
of the *Admonitio generalis* of 789 is characteristic of this outlook, for it repeats a number of suggestive terms and phrases
such as *"populus Dei", "intra ecclesiasticae firmitatis muros"*

---

[14] PL 214, 1133 AB; reproduced in the *Decretales,* C. 13, X, IV, 17.
[15] See J. Rupp, *L'idée de Chrétienté dans la pensée pontificale des
origines à Innocent III* (Paris, 1939), p. 111.
[16] *Admonitio generalis* of 789, Ch. 81. Even earlier by Pépin, Synod
of Ver. in 755, can. 14.
[17] See U. Stutz, "Das Karolingische Zehntgebot," in *Zeitschrift f.
Rechtsgesch. Germ. Abt.* 29 (1908), pp. 180ff.

and *"intra paternas sanctiones se conteneant"*. The Christian social order is a closed world that vigorously defends its internal homogeneity. To be sure, the kingdom of Charlemagne, like that of Otto in the 10th century, did expand its frontiers and thus was missionary in one sense. But it was missionary in the way that emperors are, using warfare and calling the People of God to battle with the words of the Old Testament.[18] We find the same thing again with the Crusades and with Spain's colonial expansion during the 16th century.[19]

These Old Testament citations were so interwoven into any and every attempt to fashion a People of God within the context and structures of political society that we find them once again in the various efforts at reform or reformation in the 16th century. This is quite aside from the many Old Testament allusions used to justify force against "dangerous" aberrations. We find these references wherever an attempt is made to fashion a People of God or a city of God, and to ward off dangers. The history of Puritanism has much to tell us on this score.

Seeds of Change

Lay people, particularly kings and emperors, often maintained these sacred categories to their own advantage. But the initiatives among the clergy to bring about a distinction of domains helped to create a lay society and to eventually desacralize it entirely. Paradoxically enough, the vigorous action of Gregory VII contributed greatly to this process.[20] In the great

[18] See, for example, Hincmar, *De regis persona et regio ministerio* (c. 873), c. 10: PL 125, 841f. See the references in my *Ecclésiologie du Haut Moyen Age* (Paris, 1968), pp. 287ff.

[19] The Crusades: P. Alphandéry, "Les citations bibliques chez les historiens de la Première Croisade," in *Rev. Hist. des Religions* 99 (1929), pp. 139-57; P. Rousset, *Les origines et les caractères de la première croisade* (Neuchâtel, 1945), pp. 89-99. 16th century: Martin Fernandez de Enciso (in 1513) justifies the Spanish conquests by referring to the Exodus and the taking of Jericho; L. Hanke, *Colonisation et conscience chrétienne au XVIe siècle* (Paris, 1957), pp. 30-31.

[20] A fact stressed by several German historians: A. Brackmann, in *Histor. Zeitsch.* 149 (1934), pp. 229-39; G. Kallen and A. Mayer-Pfannholz, "Heinrich IV und Gregor VII im Lichte der Geistesgeschichte,"

struggle between the priesthood and the empire, Henry IV held faithfully to the old Germanic notion about the sacred character of the emperor; for his own benefit, he wished to maintain the lack of distinction imbedded in the Carolingian concepts of the *populus Dei* and the *ecclesia,* where the emperor was the *head* of both.[21] Gregory VII, on the other hand, claimed certain rights for the Church alone, and thus fostered the creation of rights peculiar to the terrestrial city.[22]

As we know, this crisis found a solution in the Concordat of Worms (September 23, 1122). The way to this solution had been paved by several people: more remotely by Wason of Liège, and more immediately by Guy de Ferrare. But it was Yves of Chartres (d. 1116) in particular who desacramentalized the sacred aspect of kingship, for he made a distinction between the sacraments proper and certain signs that had purely human and psychological reality.[23] For Yves of Chartres, investiture is a juridic fact rather than a sacred action (*"cum hoc nullam vim sacramenti generat": Epist. 60*). This was a salutary step, and the bishop of Chartres was undoubtedly helped here by the existence of a nascent *philosophical* stirring in his city. For the budding philosophical movement was attempting to desacralize nature and to make it an object of scientific study and rational interpretation.[24]

---

in *Zeitschr. für deutsche Geistesgeschichte* 2 (1936), pp. 153-65; "Die Wende von Canossa," in *Hochland* 30/2 (1932-33), pp. 385-404.

[21] With Henry, such partisans as Benzo d'Alba; then, under Urban II, the monk of Hersfeld, author of *De unitate ecclesiae conservanda.*

[22] G. Ladner claims to see, in Gregory VII, a transition from the older notion of the secular power (a function existing *within* the *ecclesia,* as two eyes in one body) to the notion of the secular power as distinct from the *ecclesia* but not outside *christianitas,* of which the pope remains the head. See his "The Concepts of 'Ecclesia' and 'Christianitas' and Their Relation to the Idea of Papal 'Plenitudo Potestatis' from Gregory VII to Boniface VIII," in *Sacerdozio e Regno da Gregorio VII a Bonifacio VIII* (Rome, 1954), pp. 47-78.

[23] Cf. H. Hoffmann, "Ivo von Chartres und die Lösung des Investiturproblems," in *Deutsches Archiv* 15 (1959), pp. 393-490; R. Sprandel, *Ivo von Chartres und seine Stellung in der Kirchengeschichte* (Stuttgart, 1962), pp. 31ff.

[24] See M.-D. Chenu, *La Théologie au XIIe siècle* (Paris, 1957), pp. 19f.

This philosophical movement grew wings when the Scholastics had at their disposal the rational instruments provided by Aristotle's newly introduced works. It became even more decisive with regard to our present question when they were in possession of Aristotle's *Politics* (1260).[25] There they found a theory of the State (to use a modern expression), where the latter was defined in terms of a *temporal* common good that was peculiar to it. This common good had to be subordinated to man's ultimate supernatural goal, to be sure, but it was independent and autonomous in its own sphere. In the work of Thomas Aquinas and John of Paris we find a sketchy outline of the doctrine that would become the teaching of Leo XIII. Their use of Old Testament texts is quite remarkable and noteworthy, and John of Paris provides a lucid and trenchant critique of the abusive interpretations made by the hierocrats.[26] He does it by providing a more literal and historical interpretation of the original meaning.

In general, the Scholastics realized well enough the originality of the new law vis-à-vis the old law. Thomas Aquinas was outstanding in this respect. His use and interpretation of Deuteronomy 17 is remarkable when compared with that of Innocent III in *Per venerabilem*. Thomas cites verses 14-20 as a brief portrait of what a prince should be (I/II, q. 105, a. 1), in accordance with the common usage. But he gives verses 7-13 their historical Old Testament sense (a. 2, ad 7): The Israelite people were under the special rule and care of God, and that is why they lived under a positively theocratic regime; but this regime is no longer ours (a. 1, ad 1). Thomas also cites the *"venite ad sacerdotes"* of verse 9, but in a judiciary rather than a hierocratic sense.

[25] G. de Lagarde devotes the first and second volumes of his six-volume work, *La naissance de l'esprit laique au déclin du Moyen Age*, to a "Bilan du XIIIe siècle" (³1956) and to the "Secteur social de la Scolastique" (²1958), where the Aristotelianism of the Scholastics is well indicated.

[26] See J. Leclerq, *Jean de Paris et l'ecclésiologie du XIIIe siècle* (Paris, 1942), pp. 45f.

Of course, we do not want to turn St. Thomas into a man of the 20th century or a modern secularist. It would take time for temporal society to shed sacralization, or, rather, a sacral type of Christianity. But Chenu's remarks on Vatican Council II's "consecration" of the world are well taken. He notes that it is no longer a question of a clerical type of sacralization. Vatican Council II's consecration simply means that we are to use the world in a way that is acceptable to God. In more than one text, the Council solemnly recognized the autonomy of the world in its own sphere, thus acknowledging its lay and secular character.[27]

II

TRANSCENDENTAL PARADIGMS AND SOCIAL CHANGE

Antiquity and the Middle Ages were hardly revolutionary times, but this is not to say that we do not find rebellious movements during those epochs. In the 4th and 5th centuries we had the Circumcellion movement, which was associated with African Donatism. There was the creation of the communes in the latter part of the 11th century, often against the expressed wishes of churchmen. Lay movements espousing poverty fill the history of three centuries, from the Pataria of Milan (middle of the 11th century) to the English Lollards. These movements were often anti-hierarchical and anti-ecclesiastical, bearing witness to latent class struggles.[28] There were also peasant uprisings, particularly the one which occurred in the middle of the

[27] M.-D. Chenu, "Les laïcs et la 'consecratio mundi'," in *L'Eglise de Vatican II*, published under the direction of G. Barauna (Paris, 1966), pp. 1035-52. My study, "Situation du 'sacré' en régime chrétien," in *La Liturgie après Vatican II* (Paris, 1967), pp. 385-403. On the autonomy of the temporal, see Vatican II, *Gaudium et spes*, nn. 36, 42, 56, 76; *Lumen gentium*, n. 36; *Apostolicam actuositatem*, n. 7.

[28] See J. Le Goff, *La civilisation de l'Occident médiéval* (Paris, 1965), esp. pp. 367-77; H. Pirenne, *Histoire économique de l'Occident médiéval* (1951), pp. 336ff.

14th century, the revolts of 1323 and 1391 in Flanders, and the revolt of 1381 in England. We also have the figure of Jan Hus in Bohemia, and the various upheavals inspired by his teaching.

Yet, granting all that, we can still make three pertinent observations: (1) the European Middle Ages saw few social movements that could properly be called revolutionary; (2) such movements were usually opposed or actively put down by the Church; (3) the theologians talked about the right of resistance and offered a theology of intestinal warfare (*seditio*), but they did not propose a theology of revolution. For all its contemporaneity, the *Dictionnaire de Théologie catholique* has no articles on "revolt" or "revolution".

Individual Morality and the Tyrant

The great ages of faith did show a keen concern for justice, but this concern seems to have focused mainly on the *moral* question of personal sin and personal virtue. It was limited to the consideration of individual and personal uprightness, and it never reached the point of proposing to change the conditions and situations that were the sources of injustice. That, at least, is the conclusion we would offer on the basis of such illustrative facts as the following:

1. There was the canonically sanctioned practice of refusing the liturgical offerings of sinners, and donations or bequests that derived from wrongdoing.[29] In the Middle Ages we also hear the question posed: Can a man offer ill-gotten goods as alms? In the end, the ill-gotten goods were confiscated anyway,[30] but people did not go so far as to suggest that the root causes of the evil should be tackled.

[29] *Const. Apostol.* III c. 8, n. 1 (Funk I, pp. 196-97); IV c. 5-9 (pp. 225ff.); Council of Elvira, 300-03 or 313-14, c. 28 (PL 84, 305); St. Basil refused to accept the offering of a crooked prefect (Gregory of Nazianzen, *Orat.* 43, c. 52: PG 36, 564); St. Augustine, *Sermo* 355, 3-5 (PL 39, 1571-72); *Statuta Ecclesiae antiqua,* c. 69 (Paris 1960), p. 91 = Gennade of Marseille, in 476-485; Council of Auxerré of 585 (578), c. 17 (Mansi 9, 913); ninth Council of Toledo, 675, c. 4 (Mansi 11, 27).

[30] The fourth Council of Toledo, for example, deposed Swinthila and

2. We have the example of various holy people who were confronted with this question of using and enjoying ill-gotten goods. A Cistercian abbot was appointed bishop of Ivrée by Innocent III, but he fled from his new appointment as soon as he discovered that his domain included some assets of questionable provenience.[31] On the advice of her spiritual director, Elizabeth of Thuringia avoided using royal goods in cases where she suspected theft; she even went so far as to refuse certain dishes at mealtime for the same reason.[32]

The Middle Ages also proclaimed the right, and even the duty, of resisting a "tyrant", and it proclaimed this right with remarkable force and persistence. It had a pretty precise notion of what a tyrant was—a notion that derived from Aristotle, and from Socrates and the Romans (Cicero) through the Church Fathers.[33] Resistance to a tyrant, which could go as far as tyrannicide, was grounded on the notion that only conformity to justice conferred legitimacy on a ruler. In short, such resistance was associated with individual rulers who lacked objective uprightness; it was not our modern notion of revolution at all.

F. Kern (see footnote 33) points up one of the important traits that differentiates the two views. The right of resistance to a tyrant was foreseen and provided for in the unwritten constitution of medieval society, while none of our modern constitutions provide for the right of revolution. Modern man is less concerned about personal, ethical conformity to a transcendent truth; he is

---

confiscated his possessions "*quas de miserorum sumptibus hauserunt*" (A. K. Ziegler, *Church and State In Visigothic Spain* [Washington, 1930], p. 98).

[31] See H. Tillmann, *Papst Innocenz III* (Bonn, 1954), p. 253, n. 119.

[32] Deposition of Ysentrude: *Dicta quattuor ancillarum* (K. A. Huyskens, *Hist. Jahrbuch* 28 [1907], p. 813). The same desire not to profit "*de praeda et exactione pauperum*" led Elizabeth to leave Wartburg after the death of her husband: deposition of Irmingarde (p. 827).

[33] There is an enormous bibliography on the notion of the tyrant and on the right of resistance to him. We shall just mention three works: F. Kern, *Gottesgnadentum und Widerstandsrecht im früheren Mittelalter* (Leipzig, 1915); *Widerstandsrecht und Grenzen der Staatsgewalt*, edited by B. Pfister and G. Hilsmann (Berlin, 1956); O. Jaszi and J. D. Lewis, *Against the Tyrant: The Tradition and Theory of Tyrannicide* (Glenoe, 1957).

more sensitive to economic, social or political conditions that he regards as oppressive. Moreover, the medieval theologians saw legitimate insurrection as a rebellion against a leader, a personal embodiment of authority, not as a radical overturning of the social order.[34] Since these men were just as intelligent as we are, we might well try to explain what kept them from developing the revolutionary stance that is becoming more and more characteristic in our day.

The Divine Order

To begin with, the people of the Middle Ages strongly felt that a fixed order, ordained by divine providence, existed in society as well as in the physical universe. The *institutio regni* was ordained to follow the *institutio mundi*.[35] Their dominant world view was a cosmological and a cosmocentric one, rather than an historical one centered on man and his designs. By imitating cosmic models, the secular city would conform to the order set up by divine reason.

It is quite justifiable to look for the roots of this conviction in Plato and the Stoics.[36] But we might also point to a vaguer, less well defined feeling that had found lofty expression among countless peoples from antiquity on. In the Middle Ages, this feeling was concretely embodied in the institution of estates (*ordines*).[37] In the great world machine, each person had his own proper place with its rights and duties. He belonged to a certain group that was firmly integrated into an overall hierarchical

[34] So says St. Thomas where he broaches the question (*In II Sent.*, d. 44 q. 2, a. 2; II/II q. 42, esp. a. 2 ad 3; q. 104, a. 5 and 6); Henri of Ghent (*Quodl.* XIV, q. 8) and Peter Aureoli (*In IV Sent.*, d. 36), cited by G. de Lagarde, *op. cit.* II, pp. 195 and 299.

[35] "Optimum videtur regis officium a forma regiminis naturalis assumere," Thomas Aquinas, *De regim. princip.* I, 12.

[36] See the enlightening remarks of H. Schmidt, "Politics and Christology: Historical Background," in *Concilium* 36 (1968), pp. 72-84.

[37] See Ruth Mohl, *The Three Estates in Medieval and Renaissance Literature* (New York, 1933), especially pp. 277-83 (on divine origin) and 332 (not changing one's estate); cf. my study, "Les laïcs et l'ecclesiologie des 'ordines' chez les théologiens des XIe et XIIe siècles," in *I laici nella 'Societas christiana' dei secoli XIe XII* (Milan, 1968), pp. 83-117; in particular, for what follows, the texts and references cited on pp. 113ff.

order. As the *Hortus deliciarum* put it, men would find salvation *"per obedientiam in suis ordinibus"*. And the worst sin, the root of all sins, was pride (*superbia*). The proud man refused to stay in his proper place; instead of fitting himself into the overall order, he egotistically sought his own exaltation.[38]

This ideology obviously imposed a certain social rigidity in the name of a sacred order. Emancipation movements and efforts to overthrow the existing order were readily judged to be sinful in such an overall context.[39]

Allusions to transcendental and heavenly models were quite normal in medieval society, imbued as it was with an exemplarist and essentialist spirit. It was "platonism for the people", as Nietzsche scornfully remarked. One of the most forthright examples of this spirit is to be found in the *De universo* of William of Auvergne (d. 1248): To undermine the social order on earth was to attack heaven itself! The theocrats did not hesitate to make frequent analogies between the ecclesiastical hierarchy and the celestial hierarchy. Such analogies were challenged by the measured analyses of such men as Thomas Aquinas and John of Paris. But it was the radical criticism of two truly revolutionary thinkers, Marsilius of Padua (d. c. 1342) and William of Ockham (d. c. 1349) that focused the spotlight on new values and ushered in the spirit of modern times.[40]

[38] On the role of *superbia* in the social and historical outlook of the post-Augustine Middle Ages, see E. Bernheim, *Mittelalterliche Zeitanschauungen in ihrem Einfluss auf Politik und Geschichtschreibung*, Part I (Tübingen, 1918). Compare the remarks of R. Garaudy, "What Does a Non-Christian Expect of the Church in Matters of Social Morality?" in *Concilium* 35 (1968), pp. 24-45.

[39] G. B. Ladner, "Religious Renewal and Ethnic-Social Pressures as Forms of Life in Christian History," in *Theology of Renewal* II (Montreal, 1968), pp. 328-57. Citing numerous references (p. 342, n. 39), he illustrates the fact that the creation of communes was often seen as a rebellion against the established order. As I see it, the texts do not actually say so much.

[40] One would do well to read W. Kölmel, "Typik und Atypik: Zum Geschichtsbild der kirchenpolitischen Publizistik (11-14 Jahrh.)," in *Speculum Historiale* (Freiburg-Munich, 1965), pp. 277-302; *idem, Wilhélm Ockham und seine kirchenpolitischen Schriften* (Essen, 1962).

This does not mean that their thoughts coincided. Marsilius argued in true Aristotelian fashion, moving from *facts and things*. He also had a certain yearning for a return to the primitive Church, and he rejected the hierocratic appeal to the Old Testament and Deuteronomy (*Defensor pacis* II, III, IX). William of Ockham, on the other hand, presented a metaphysics that stressed God's absolute freedom and his independence from any and all law. He also presented an anthropology centered around the free individual person, and proclaimed a spirituality of evangelical freedom that showed little concern for the demands of good order. Here was a truly revolutionary principle, leaving room for criticism and even rejection of a de-divinized order.

On the whole, the recourse to transcendent models favored social immobility. But it is only fair to note that this emphasis could also inspire revolutionary transformations at times. The reform movement that took place between the 11th and 13th centuries was an historical fact of great scope and importance. Based on the ideals of the primitive Church, it involved more than spiritual and moral reform. Through the action of Gregory VII,[41] it also tackled social relationships and the economic status of the clergy.

Aversion to Innovation

Another factor also helps to explain the non-revolutionary cast of the medieval centuries. The people of that period, like those of antiquity, strongly felt that the older and more stable a thing was, the more truth it contained.[42] The ideal was not to innovate in any way. The heretic was essentially an "innovator",

[41] See G. Miccoli, "Ecclesiae primitivae forma," in *Chiesa Gregoriana* (Florence, 1966), pp. 225-99, esp. pp. 244ff. See also D. Zema, "Reform Legislation in the Eleventh Century and Its Economic Import," in *Catholic Historical Review* 27 (1941), pp. 1ff.; *idem*, "Economic Reorganization of the Roman See during the Gregorian Reform," in *Studi Gregoriani* I (Rome, 1947), pp. 137-68.

[42] See J. Spörl, "Das Alte und das Neue," in *Histor. Jahrb.* 50 (1930), pp. 301f.

and nothing could be worse. People were expected and obliged to follow the traditions of their forefathers.

This ideal was not total or all-pervasive. Medieval men could be highly creative, and some people were greatly praised for their novel ideas. But the basic aim was to give new shape and vitality to old ideas; it was *reformatio, renovatio* and *legis emendatio*. Modern man, by contrast, sees greater truth in what has not yet come to be; greater truth and better things lie ahead in the future. The innovator and the heretic now enjoy prestige and hero-worship, as Kierkegaard once noted.[43]

Notion of Historicity

One might well suggest another factor here. It is just possible that medieval man had a different outlook on human historicity than we do today. As Schillebeeckx puts it: "Today, in contrast with 'medieval' man, we know that the social 'establishment' is not a divine creation but a cultural and man-made situation which can be dealt with and reformed." [44]

The ancients did have a strong sense of the *mutabilitas* of earthly realities, and this was a real category in their philosophy or theology of history (e.g., in Otto of Freising's work). But this mutability did not present human historicity as the framework and locale for man's creativity; it was seen as a mark of man's frailty and finiteness, of his imperfection vis-à-vis an ideally stable order. Thomas Aquinas did have a more positive outlook on time and human efforts toward self-fulfillment, as M. Seckler has shown; but even Thomas sets these efforts in the framework of personal ethics and individual effort, rather than in the broader framework of a societal life based on material conditions and historical dimensions.

---

[43] S. Kierkegaard, *The Sickness unto Death.*

[44] E. Schillebeeckx, "The Magisterium and the World of Politics," in *Concilium* 36 (1968), p. 30. Note also his footnote reference (n. 18) to the work of H. Freyer, *Theorie des gegenwärtigen Zeitalters* (Stuttgart, ²1963).

Even to this day we find traces of the older outlook in Catholic thought. Its "latent anthropology" [45] contains elements of a-temporal essentialism and older sacralism; it operates on a vague providentialist tendency that fails to give full recognition to man's initiatives and his historicity.

[45] Houtart-Hambye, "Socio-Political Implications of Vatican Council II," in *Concilium* 36 (1968), pp. 85-96.

Hans Bornewasser/*Goirle, Netherlands*

State and Politics from the Renaissance to the French Revolution

I

THE PRACTICAL REALITY IN NORTHERN ITALY
AND MACHIAVELLI'S THEORY

The modern State was born in northern Italy, where it was baptized with the name "stato" in the 15th century, or, rather, was given that name. For the idea of baptism, as the bestowing of a Christian sign and the consciousness of a Christian vocation, was alien to the small city-states that prized themselves out of the medieval feudal framework. The first purely secular small States arose within Christendom through the vacuum created by the medieval struggle between pope and emperor. Their prince was not anointed with sacred oil as the seal on his position, and their mutual relations were not determined by a hierarchical and feudal consecration.[1] Here "the State" was created "as a work of art", as Jacob Burckhardt pointed out more than a century ago.[2] Internally, this State was a "work of art", in the sense of a consciously thought out creation; externally, pressed by necessity, it learned the art of maintaining itself in the interplay of power-politics.

[1] Garrett Mattingly, *Renaissance Diplomacy* (London, ³1963), pp. 56-57.

[2] J. Burckhardt, *Die Cultur der Renaissance in Italien* (1860), Ch. I.

Condottieri who had seized a throne, minor or major tyrants, and more important princely families like the Gonzagas in Mantua, the Sforzas in Milan and the Medici in Florence, constituted, together with the older powers of Venice and the papal States, the first and still extremely fluid system of political States in Western European history. Within each State, absolutism was practiced in its most usurping and illegitimate form. In its relations with the outside, it was dominated by the "reason of States", a code of behavior rooted in exclusive self-interest and formulated in purely rational terms, which guided its unblushing opportunism in the political relations with others.

Niccolò Machiavelli (d. 1527) was the acute observer of what took place in northern Italy during the Renaissance. The most famous of his historical political writings was *Il Principe* (*The Prince*). He was more than the contemporary historian who only wrote down what he had seen and learned. He meant to write "something useful" and investigate "how a prince ought to behave toward his subjects and friends".[3] Here he had in mind a powerful Medici prince who would know how to achieve unity and balance of power. And so this controversial work became a political textbook to guide princes in general.

This constituted a definite breakaway from the "mirrors for princes" that pullulated in the past. In those "mirrors" the prince represented God in political matters and was the sacred zenith of an ideally organized political structure. The doctrine of political conduct had been part of a Scholastic philosophy and theology which started by assuming an ideal reality, rooted in God's order. Indeed, according to St. Paul, all power was from God. Consequently as the bearer of secular power, the prince had to fulfill his task as appointed by God and was responsible to God. In contrast, Machiavelli tried to work out an empirical and rational stystem by which a prince would be able to defend an artificially maintained State against dangers from within and without. He did not deny what Scholastic thinkers had laid down as the function of State and prince within the God-willed

[3] *Il Principe,* Ch. XV.

hierarchical order. He simply started from the other end, from the reality as he found it. For him, politics was an independent business. It was in no way dependent on what, according to him, was formulated in principles that were alien to life and based on a theocratic authority.

This did not mean that Machiavelli had no room for religion in his politics. On the contrary, religion was a powerful weapon in the control of social forces. But the prince would only use it as a means for his own ends: the most powerful confirmation of the States's own independent and secular interests.[4]

Machiavelli saw the struggle of those small, modern, secularized States all around him. His interest lay with the first actual process of secularization which was still confined to a geographically limited territory. In our own time, we can see this now as an anticipation of what was going to take place during the following centuries against a European and colonial background. This Florentine thinker, matured in experience, distilled the theory of what in fact was happening in a unique historical situation, and so he created a certain legitimation of it. For him the traditional theological and philosophical foundation of the State, brought in from outside, had to yield to an empirical and rational foundation from within. The *esperienza delle cose,* the experience of things as they are, was the main force of his theory. He was the first to put together the elements of a purely secular theory of the State. The result, therefore, was not so much a well-ordered doctrine as a motley quantity of observations and practical maxims. The harsh, unscrupulous struggle between the threatened small "powers" was reflected in Machiavelli's textbook for princes in an extremely unscrupulous manner. A one-sided secular theory followed an historically unique secular practice.[5]

[4] F. Meinecke, *Die Idee der Staatsräson in der neueren Geschichte* (Munich, ²1960), Ch. I, esp. pp. 39f.

[5] E. Cassirer, *The Myth of the State* (New Haven, ³1950), pp. 129-62; H. Lutz, *Ragione di stato und Christliche Staatsethik im 16. Jahrhundert* (Münster, 1961); W. Schweitzer, *Der entmythologisierte Staat* (Gütersloh, 1968), pp. 65-76.

II
FROM A "SUFFERING CHRISTENDOM" (CHRISTIANITAS AFFLICTA) TO A RATIONAL BALANCE OF POWER

At the end of the Middle Ages the politically pre-conceived image of Christendom had lost its sheen. The rise of separate national States had been weakened into the much vaguer image of a religious bond between all Christian European States. The Hapsburg emperor of the Holy Roman Empire had become primarily a dynastic rival of other princes. The emperor's traditional function of preserving peace and justice within the whole of Western Christendom had been pushed into the background. The idea of an "empire of Christians" flickered for a last moment during the reign of Charles V (1519-55). Under this concept, one prince, now backed by the machine of a centralized power, was to wield a European Christian supremacy. His great rival, Francis I of France (1515-47), also cherished this notion when he put forward his candidacy for the emperorship whose function it would be to protect a "suffering Christendom" wounded and threatened by Reformers and Turks. As late as the middle of the 16th century a Venetian diplomat could still write that the conflict between the Houses of Hapsburg and Valois was partly determined by a religious universalism, the struggle for the supremacy over the whole of Christendom.[6]

At the same time, however, the existing secular and dynastic contrasts proved to be an effective countercheck. Charles V, intent on world power, was a lord over an empire where the sun never set, and he found in Francis I a disappointed opponent. As a nationalist Renaissance prince and at the same time "His Most Christian Majesty", Francis made an important contribution to the secularization of political relations. In his confusion of personal ambition and an ideal universalism, Charles V could easily think himself religiously inspired. On the other

[6] H. Lutz, *Christianitas afflicta* (Göttingen, 1964), p. 22 and *passim*.

hand, apart from the curiously secular-minded Frederick II of the 13th century, Francis I was the first great European prince to deliberately act on the basis of purely political interests.[7]

In his struggle with Charles, the French king for the first time appealed to the Turks for assistance, and so laid the foundation for a political and military alliance which was unthinkable before his time but soon became common practice in his country. Authors, mustered in his defense, stressed from the very beginning the difference between political and purely religious concerns. The former were rooted in the secular order of international law, while the latter were the business of Church law. The argument of St. Paul's contrast between Christ and Belial, used by frowning ecclesiastics, could hardly prevent two nations from cooperating on non-religious grounds. For the same reason Francis opposed Pope Alexander VI's demarcation of colonial territories in 1493 as if this were merely a matter of missionary work. Such religious implications might suit the Catholic kings of Spain who had here a political vested interest and therefore readily accepted this kind of *Roma locuta, causa finita* (Rome has spoken, the affair is finished), but the French king, "eldest son of the Church", appealed to such axioms of political autonomy as the freedom of trade and freedom of the seas, as well as the right of the first-comer.[8]

The conflict between the France of the Bourbons and the Spain of the Hapsburgs during the 17th century showed the same features and considerably hastened the secularization of the system of nation-states in Europe. The *rey católico* of Spain and the *roy très chrétien* of France were here at loggerheads, yet both were princes by the will of God and by divine right. There was, however, a vast difference between the pretensions of Philip IV with his Olivarès (d. 1645) and those of Louis XIV with his Richelieu (d. 1642). Spain waged a desperate battle which was essentially a political and economic one, by appealing to an idealistic crusade against heretics and Turks,

---

[7] J. Lecler, *L'Eglise et la souveraineté de l'Etat* (Paris, 1946), pp. 171f.
[8] *Ibid.*

while in France the new political realism was voiced by the anonymous author of the *Discours* of 1624 and by Henri de Rohan, in his *De l'Intérêt des Princes et Etats de la Chrétienté,* which appeared soon after. It has rightly been said that the war with Spain was the main secularizing factor in French politics and in the literature which sought to defend it.[9] The French authors showed up Spain's so-called holy wars as a fight for national interests dressed up in voluble religious pathos. The concrete situation led France to a practical policy based on national interest, and political theory supported this.

The starting point was not the abstract, ideal State, but the European situation of rising absolute States, living in permanent rivalry. One began with the system of States as it operated at that time, analyzed its structure and that of the various forces which played a part in it, and in this empirical way reached a number of positive conclusions. These were not meant to be absolute norms, derived from an eternal and God-willed order, but, as Rohan said in the dedication of his work to Richelieu, as principles of government which changed according to the circumstances prevailing at the time. Richelieu himself expressed this thought in his "Political Testament" by saying that there is nothing more dangerous for a State than people who want to govern their country by maxims taken from books.[10] This clearly meant a dissociation from political philosophical ideals derived from an eternal divine order.

The publication at that time of books which treated political conduct in empirical terms shows that people began to think in terms of politics as something secular and autonomous. Here England made a particularly important contribution. The influence of Francis Bacon (d. 1626), the founder of modern empiricism, has been of paramount importance in this field. As in all his work, his political thought shows the need for an objective

[9] E. Thuau, *Raison d'Etat et pensée politique à l'époque de Richelieu* (Paris, 1966), p. 318.
[10] Quoted by R. von Albertini, *Das politische Denken in Frankreich zur Zeit Richelieus* (Marburg, 1951). Both Albertini and Thuau are important for this subject. See also Meinecke, *op. cit.,* pp. 173f.

analysis of the concrete situation, based on numerous instances. His interest in figures of population, commercial statistics, financial results, and so on, have a truly modern flavor. Later in that same century his indications were pursued and developed by Harrington in his famous *Oceana* and by Petty in his *Political Arithmetic*. According to Petty, England's position among the European States should be analyzed and improved on the basis of comparative political analysis and the geo-political description of various countries.[11]

Thus the conviction grew that politics should not be guided by abstract ideals laid down by theology and philosophy but by the practical needs of the country to be governed. This pragmatic and functional approach, deliberately secular in the sense of being independent of religious considerations in international matters, would be a good description of the factual policies pursued by Richelieu. It fits his alliances with Protestant princes, which a French Jesuit described as astonishing in its modernity.[12] A contemporary defended this by saying that it was immaterial whether one's ally was Catholic or not, since such an alliance rested solely on human law.[13]

What this human law, international law and universal human solidarity actually involved, however, was a vast problem. But those who had to rebut the accusation of indulging in Machiavellianism agreed that these elements had to be considered. A French Calvinist of the 16th century noted with horror that Machiavelli's works were as frequently read by courtiers as was the breviary by village priests.[14] To the advantage of both, and better than the other way around, one might think. The defenders of the "reason of State" fiercely objected to being identified with Machiavelli. It was a popular argument to make an essentially rather futile distinction between good and bad "rea-

[11] Cf. W. H. Greenleaf, *Order, Empiricism and Politics. Two Traditions of English Political Thought, 1500-1700* (London/New York, 1964).

[12] Lecler, *op. cit.*, p. 175.

[13] *Ibid.*, p. 177.

[14] Lutz, *Ragione* etc., *op. cit.*, p. 39.

sons of State". The conviction was that inter-State relations were not subject to the same norms as those that govern ordinary public and social life. An important point for that age was the calculating trust in rational and just political conduct: the good reputation of the prince could not be played with. Thus Richelieu, in contrast with Machiavelli, insisted that treaties once concluded should be honored "religiously", even if this seemed to go against the immediate interest of the State. The prince's reputation was also, in the political theory of the Stoic Christian thinker Lipsius (d. 1606),[15] the indispensable condition for his authority.

We may therefore conclude that, particularly during the 17th century, practical foreign policy as conducted by people who believed was detached from the religious aims and interests with which it was at first more definitely linked as a result of the Reformation. For one should not forget that in the Middle Ages many policies were pursued on the basis of regional interests in a way which was in fact more secular than in the 16th century when religious passions broke loose. Continuing the work of the late-Scholastic Spaniards Vitoria and Suárez and the Fleming Lipsius, the Dutchman Hugo de Groot laid the foundations for an international law based on a rationally developed natural law.[16] In this context a sentence from the introduction to his *De Jure belli et pacis* (1625) is often quoted: as principles of moral conduct the laws of nature retain their validity even if there were no God.[17] He himself was a believer. Some fifty years later Pufendorf, followed by Thomasius around 1700, founded a rationalistic natural law by detaching the question of international relations from any divine law.

During the same period another theory was developed in order to support the policy of securing a practical balance of power between the States of the 17th and 18th centuries. The empirical studies which set up this theory flourished during the Spanish

---

[15] Cf. G. Oestreich, "Justus Lipsius als Theoretiker des neuzeitlichen Machtstaates," in *Hist. Zeitschr.* 181 (1956).

[16] Cassirer, *op. cit.*, p. 172.

[17] "Even if we admitted, what we cannot admit without grievous wrong, that there is no God": H. Grotius, *De iure belli et pacis*, n. 11. For the meaning of this sentence, see Schweitzer, *op. cit.*, p. 145.

War of Succession. The widely used term "balance" betrays both English influence and the rather mechanical approach. The Enlightenment produced a further development in the theory of "reason of balance". It started from the ideal of the "well-balanced" man who maintains this balance in his political affairs within a cosmos that is itself balanced. The great protagonist of this theory was the diplomat Charles de Vergennes in the 1770's. In contrast with Machiavelli's pessimistic realism, this new theory not only started with an optimistic and idealistic hypothesis, but also showed how in practice European politics had already begun to think in terms of a totality of States. The interest of one's own country would therefore be best served by fitting it in with the interests of all together. In this way the secularized theory would protect the secularized practice from the constant menace of immoral egotism.[18]

III

THE MYTH OF THE "DIVINE RIGHT"
AND ITS REJECTION BY LATE-SCHOLASTICISM

The growth of the modern centralized national State went through the phase of absolute kingship. Driven by the spirit of the Renaissance and the actual development of governmental and economic obligations, energetic princes of England, France, Sweden and Spain—and soon, also, the various separate States of Germany—built their bureaucratic States. By means of a powerful army, a growing bureaucratic machinery for government, a mercantilist economy and a national culture, the separate sovereign State became at the same time an absolute State. The doctrine of the sovereign State was for the first time formulated by Jean Bodin in a way which became classic. He has been called the protagonist of the contemporary secularizing currents of the

---

[18] For the "balance of power", see E. von Vietsch, *Das europäische Gleichgewicht* (Leipzig, 1942); E. Vose Gulick, *Europe's Classical Balance of Power* (Ithaca, 1955); G. Zeller, "Le principe d'équilibre dans la politique internationale avant 1789," in *Rev. Hist.* 205 (1956).

age. He sought to overcome the religious quarrels which tore his country apart by putting himself above denominational conflicts. He built up his political doctrine with a realistic sense of the concrete changing circumstances. In his *Six Livres de la République* (1576) he described the power of the absolute prince as supreme and not bound by laws (*summa in cives legibusque soluta potestas*). The sovereign had to act according to justice, and this, so to speak, made God's will and the welfare of the State coincide.[19] An experimental understanding and the persistent rational analysis of the all-powerful State as the body which creates order, prosperity and justice characterizes the theories which accompanied the growth of the sovereign State. The prince's sovereignty was almost geometrically defined: according to one 17th-century author it was as indivisible as the geometrical point.[20] In this rising absolutism the State became the product of the secularizing mentality which fitted the breakthrough of the pragmatic and functional elements in the build-up of post-medieval political structures.

But to say that this absolutism was only a link in the secularizing process is but a half-truth.[21] The other half lies in what Marc Bloch said: "Absolutism was a sort of religion."[22] The sacred magic mentality which made medieval people think that the king could cure the sick, particularly those suffering from glandular diseases such as scrofula, persisted during the period of absolutism—in England until the beginning of the 18th century, in France until the last Bourbon before the Revolution. In order to persuade the ordinary people of the legitimacy of the absolute king, the old idea of a sacred kingship was deliberately

[19] For the role of Bodin, see P. Mesnard, *L'essor de la philosophie politique au XVIe siècle* (Paris, 1936), pp. 538f.; G. Scharffenorth, *Römer 13 in der Geschichte des politischen Denkens* (Heidelberg, 1964), pp. 204f.; Greenleaf, *op. cit.*, pp. 125-41.

[20] M. Göhring, *Weg und Sieg der modernen Staatsidee in Frankreich* (Tübingen, 1947), p. 105.

[21] Cf. W. Mommsen, "Zur Beurteilung des Absolutismus," in *Hist. Zeitsch.* 158 (1938), p. 55: "For the great process of secularization which, during the centuries, overcame the Middle Ages step for step, the question of absolutism is particularly important."

[22] M. Bloch, *Les rois thaumaturges* (Strasbourg/Paris, 1924), p. 345.

revived. And so the image of the king continued to live as that of a miracle-working king, the bearer of a political-religious charisma. The critical thought of the intellectuals did not affect this "religion of the king" (*religion royale*). It was, for instance, not considered to do any harm when a friend of Montaigne's pointed out that according to ancient belief King Pyrrhus could cure illness with his big toe.[23] The position of the "Most Christian King" was more assured by the ordinary man's trusting belief in the king's God-hallowed function than by any theory.

But even at this level a theory was formulated. This proceeded from a one-sided, absolutist refinement of St. Paul's ("There is no authority except from God") to the so-called "divine right" of kings. The first and most consistent upholder of this theory was himself a king, James I of England, whom Henry IV of France liked to call the "wisest fool on the throne". According to him, kings are not only God's vicars on earth, seated on God's throne, but are called "gods" by God himself. The divine attributes are applicable to the king, since he exercises a kind of divine power on earth. He decides matters of life and death; he makes or breaks the power of his subjects, even bishops or noblemen; he rules them all in body and soul. In all this he is only responsible to God.[24]

While in England this theoretical sacralization of the king fitted in naturally with a national Church and its royal supremacy, in France it displayed features of Gallicanism. There, too, from the beginning of the 17th century, the civilian theorists maintained that royal power was absolute and sacred. The theory of divine right (*droit divin*) stressed that the king of France had received his mission and consecration directly from God, so that only God (and not the Church of Rome!) could judge his actions. As the last great defender of this divine right, Bossuet finished the monopolization of this theory by Gallicanism in

---

[23] P. E. Schramm, *Der König von Frankreich* I (Weimar, 1960), p. 270.

[24] J. N. Figgis, *The Divine Right of the Kings* (Cambridge, ²1922); H. Deimann, *Die Doktrin vom göttlichen Rechte der Könige bei Jakob I. von England im 17. Jahrhundert* (Cologne, 1957).

1682. According to him, the king is the absolute source of law in the State, and like its creator, this source is of divine origin.[25]

This divine right of kings contained a curious contradiction. For all its formal religious appearance, it was in fact meant to provide backing for the secular interests of the State. In spite of its sacred halo it was meant as propaganda for a policy based on plain "reason of State". Therefore, in spite of its affinity with the medieval kingship "by the grace of God", it was something profoundly different.[26] In the Middle Ages it had always been linked with the right to revolt, because this "grace of God" was still coupled with a certain sense of the sovereignty of the people. This neutralizing factor was lost with the one-sided application of this "grace of God" to the absolutism of the modern State. The same holds for the balancing forces in the universal Church, which, in accordance with the legalistic tradition of Roman law, were as far as possible deprived of their effectiveness. In this divine right of kings the national Church and the absolute State were inextricably knitted together in a bundle of essentially secular interests.

It was against this that the later Scholastic theologians, among whom the Italian Jesuit Robert Bellarmine (d. 1621) was the most prominent, reacted so strongly. Thomist theology had taught Bellarmine that ecclesiastical power was wholly based on divine law and came directly from God. Secular power, however, was in origin indeed willed by God and derived from God but achieved by human planning and human choice. The positive cooperation of the people in the setting up of a concrete political order is even more strongly emphasized by Bellarmine than by St. Thomas.[27] In the same way, the Spanish Scholastics of the

    [25] Cf. Albertini and Göhring, already referred to, and S. Skalweit, "Das Herrscherbild des 17. Jahrhunderts," in *Hist. Zeitsch.* 184 (1957).
    [26] O. Brunner, "Vom Gottesgnadentum zum monarchischen Prinzip," in *Das Königtum. Seine geistige und rechtlichen Grundlagen* (Mainauvorträge, 1954), p. 291.
    [27] F. X. Arnold, *Die Staatslehre des Kardinals Bellarmin* (Munich, 1934), pp. 196f.

16th century, like Vitoria, Soto and Suárez, had left no room for an absolute divine kingship in their theory about the agreement that had to exist between king and people. In spite of all their static metaphysical ideas about man and society, these theologians clearly saw the distinction between Church and State at a time when the secular was absolutized and deified while religion was made to serve secular opportunism,[28] just as in the Middle Ages the political teaching of Aristotle and Thomas had defended an autonomy of political conduct which was frowned upon by the Church.

Bellarmine went even farther in his assertion of the State's right to autonomy. Politics was a concern of this world and had its own ends and means to achieve those ends, for its purpose was to achieve the highest level of temporal welfare for the whole community. Nevertheless, his theory of the indirect power of the pope subordinated a non-sacred, secular and political world to the spiritual, sacred power of the international Church of Rome. Religious life, being of a higher order, was above secular life. If the pope thought that spiritual interests, with eternal consequences, were in danger, he was entitled to intervene in secular affairs. This meant in fact that the Church itself could decide whether such was the case, and therefore had the last word. This has rightly been called a kind of "reason of Church", the counterpart of the king's "reason of State".[29]

In Bellarmine, the fierce opponent of James I, the secular autonomous State found a dubious advocate. His theory was meant to demythologize a sacred kingship but in fact remained rooted in a supernatural interpretation of all social structures. It offered a norm-giving theology of the State, based on metaphysics, and attributed to the Church the power of ultimate supervision over the State.

[28] B. Hamilton, *Political Thought in Sixteenth-Century Spain* (Oxford, 1963).

[29] The expression is H. de Lubac's, quoted by Lecler, *op. cit.*, p. 104. See also J. C. Murray, "St. Robert Bellarmine on the Indirect Power," in *Theol. Studies* IX (1948), pp. 491-535.

IV

THE SIGNIFICANCE OF PROTESTANTISM

Up until now we have left the Reformers out of our discussion of the secularization of State and politics. Those who are aware of the way in which modern authors (as opposed to writers of the last century) see the reformer rather as a contemporary obstacle to the "total secularization of thought and sentiment" [30] will find this hardly surprising. Was Luther not above all God's prophetic messenger, the reformer of Church and theology? And are not all human phenomena and developments given their meaning and function by theology in the theocracy of Calvin for whom theology had the last word in the guidance of human conduct? [31]

This is nevertheless hardly the whole explanation of the influence exercised by the Reformation on politics. Luther's paradoxical teaching of the two kingdoms, linked with that of the two "regimes", aimed at setting secular power free from spiritual power, although circumstances forced him to attribute an ecclesiastical function to the secular prince. The function of authority in the political sphere and a Christian's conduct in this world he saw clearly as a rational and pragmatic activity within this world. In Luther's mind the sinful world is indeed of God but has nothing in common with him; it cannot be evangelized or christened. Although the prince has a divine mandate, he does not apply a Christian policy because there is no such thing. All he has to do is to use his political understanding. Thus Luther wanted to see the war against the Turks as a political conflict that originated in political and military needs. One would confuse God's spiritual regime with his worldly one if one turned the war into a crusade. According to Luther's interpretation of St. Paul's letter

[30] G. Ritter, *Luther, Gestalt und Tat* (we are not here considering Gogarten's individual view of the theology of secularization).

[31] Cf. A. Biéler, *La pensée économique et sociale de Calvin* (Geneva, 1959).

to the Romans, secular power must not be obstructed by spiritual power because it has its own divine authority and mission.[32]

In practice this meant for the Lutheran States that there the secular power of the prince could freely develop its absolute nature. Luther's thought encouraged the spread of absolutism because there was no opposition from the Church. When, around 1700, Thomasius legitimized an existing power structure on a purely natural basis because of his purely rational interpretation of natural law, there was no longer any need for support from Scripture. Without it, absolutism could continue to operate in its secularized ways, and a so-called "established Church" (*Staatskirchentum*) of a utilitarian kind could easily fit in with that. This is of course not what Luther had in mind, but is nevertheless connected with it.[33]

Calvinism started from another angle, and therefore produced other results. In contrast with Luther, Calvin emphasized the Christian significance of the State over which he cast the splendor of God's majesty. God's will is law in political life. The political order is there "because of sin". The authorities are bound by the Word of Scripture from which we can derive what God decrees. The distinction between a natural and a supernatural order was alien to Calvin. This meant in practice that for the Calvinist the Church must try to influence and shape the social order. Worldly authorities therefore had a religious task to fulfill. With its view of the establishment of God's kingdom on earth, early Calvinism underlined the religious element in politics.[34]

In actual fact, these Calvinistic theories about the State acted as a brake on the growing absolutism of the State. Their theocratic tendency, together with the teaching of various spheres of

[32] From the vast literature we refer to H. Bornkamm, "Luthers Lehre von den zwei Reichen im Zusammenhang seiner Theologie," in *Archiv für Reformationsgeschichte* 49 (1958), pp. 22-49, and J. van Laarhoven, "The Origin of Luther's Doctrine of the Two Kingdoms," in *Concilium* 17 (1966), pp. 50-62.

[33] Cf. W. P. Fuchs (ed.), *Staat und Kirche im Wandel der Jahrhunderte* (1966), and the bibliography given there.

[34] J. Bohatec, *Calvins Lehre von Staat und Kirche* (Aalen, ²1961); T. G. Sanders, *Protestant Concepts of Church and State* (New York, 1964), pp. 225f.

power within the State, kept the anti-absolute forces alive, sometimes to the point of revolution. This produced an insistence on constitutional behavior and so we should understand the *Vindiciae contra tyrannos* to Duplessis-Mornay (1579) and the *Politica* of Althusius (1603). In England and the American colonies the many forms of Puritanism thus created a climate in which democratic tendencies could develop. When this Calvinism began to weaken under the pressure of changing social structures and the development of science, one of the results was that, with this background, the secularization process led to a constitutional democracy. The Declaration of Independence of 1776 and the Bill of Rights in various American States can be explained in this light. Once again, we have here a development which was not directly Calvin's own creation, but is connected with him.[35]

Lutheranism in no way necessarily implied absolutism, and Calvinism did not explicitly point the way to a constitutional democracy. And yet, the secularized Lutheran State was absolute, while those whose religious formation was Calvinist were constitutionally inclined in their legal and political views. A religiously shaped historical mold would gradually be filled with non-religious ideas. And so the different approaches of Luther and Calvin to political life had a lasting and equally different effect on the secularizing process in which their followers were involved.

V

THE RATIONALIZATION OF THE STATE
AND THE DECLINE OF THE MONARCHY

Two characteristic features emerge from our discussion about the secularization of State and politics. The first is the empiri-

[35] Schweitzer, *op. cit.*, pp. 98f., shows something of the complexity of the problem. See there also the bibliographic references. That the Calvinist theorists owed much to the Spanish authors already mentioned is clear from E. Reibstein, *Johannes Althusius als Fortsetzer der Schule von Salamanca* (Karlsruhe, 1955).

cal approach to the question of the State and its domestic and foreign policies. It has become clear that the building of the State and the maintenance of its place among other States start from practical pressures and concrete historical circumstances. Along with this, but also based on this, the secular theory was developed, which means that one tried to define structures and rules of conduct in a way which cut the State loose from systems built up on Church or religion. This is particularly clear in the philosophy of natural law which was interpreted in rationalist terms, and so introduced the philosophers of the 18th century. But while new general principles were discovered, and both man and nature *as such* were considered absolute data and norms, these thinkers absolutized in a contemporary rational fashion what was in fact a combination of traditional opinions, historically inspired hypotheses and enlightened ideals. The 18th-century "philosophers" believed throughout in an ideal heavenly State within the world of the future and built their theories on this secularized "faith".[36] In the 17th and 18th centuries rationalism came to prevail over empiricism within the interplay of these secularizing factors, even in England,[37] although the physical sciences of the 18th century helped to correct what was assumed *a priori* to be "rational" and "natural". Empiricism and rationalism continued to influence each other in this secularizing process.

The philosopher of natural law, Christian Wolff, was the first in Germany to explain the State as the wholly rational product of natural human situations. His *Vernünftige Gedanken vom gesellschaftlichen Leben des Menschen* (1721) remolded the long-known theories of political treaties into a purely rational foundation of the enlightened and absolute State.[38] The fictitious social contract between the sovereign people and their prince became the soul of a sovereignty of the people which could only reinforce the power of the prince in the German States of

[36] Cf. C. L. Becker, *The Heavenly City of the 18th-Century Philosophers* (New Haven, 1932).

[37] Greenleaf, *op. cit.*, pp. 262f.

[38] F. Hartung, "Der aufgeklärte Absolutismus," in *Hist. Zeitsch.* 180 (1955), p. 23.

the 18th century. Individual human beings would willingly surrender their particular "human rights" to the prince who should do everything to raise his people to greater prosperity and higher culture. The inarticulate citizens had therefore, above all, the duty to obey what the rational and utilitarian prince prescribed for them in their own interest. Wolff provided a kind of blueprint for the rational prince in a rational State.

Enlightened absolute princes like Frederick the Great of Prussia, Charles Frederick of Baden and Joseph II of Austria were, for all their extreme absolutism, really representative of a monarchy that had lost its sacred glamor. The rational deduction of sovereignty from a pure and simple social contract meant the death knell of the old kingship by the grace of God. The prince had lost his sacred vertical link with the divine and became simply the first among his purely human equals. Unrestrained, indefatigable and constantly interfering, the enlightened absolute prince governed his people, for his people and among his people, who had bestowed all power upon him. The deliberately simple behavior of some of them as *Landesvater* (the father of the country) added to this loss of sacred glamor.[39]

While in Germany the rationalization of the State found expression in an enlightened absolutism, the pessimistic Thomas Hobbes tried to prove the need for an all-powerful State in England. The Leviathan in his work of the same name (1651) stood for the all-powerful State with an absolute prince who creates a purely earthly peace in his own tough way and without any divine mandate. In this way Hobbes secularized the absolutist tradition, without finding any acceptance for his theory in his own country. Locke, on the contrary, must be understood in the context of the "king in Parliament" of the "Glorious Revolution" (1689). While at the beginning of the century Althusius still used Scripture to argue his constitutionalism, Locke secularized this particular tradition in his *Two Treatises on Civil Government* (1690).[40]

[39] *Ibid.*, p. 40.
[40] Cf. C. J. Friedrich, *Das Zeitalter des Barock;* Schweitzer, *op. cit.*

In France the political theories of Montesquieu and Rousseau only bore fruit in the Revolution of 1789. Their rationalization of the State was only partly based on abstract argument.[41] Montesquieu particularly incorporated a wide experience in his teaching, as, for instance, in his *trias politica*, the thesis of the division of power in the State. Rousseau's *Contrat Social* (1762) display a fair amount of anthropocentric religious sentiment. When, with Louis XVI, the myth of a sacred kingship died on the guillotine, the myth of Rousseau's "general will" was meant to take shape in the terroristic regime of Robespierre. And this by itself shows already that the French Revolution was far from being the end of the secularizing process as we have tried to describe it.

See also H. W. Schneider, "Christian Theocracy and Hobbe's 'Mortal God'," in *The Sacral Kingship* (Leiden, 1959), pp. 627-32.

[41] For both these thinkers in connection with this subject, see Schweitzer, *passim;* for Rousseau, cf. F. H. Willhoite, "Rousseau's Political Religion," in *The Review of Politics* XXVII (1965), pp. 501-15.

Enrique Dussel/*Mendoza, Argentina*

From Secularization to Secularism: Science from the Renaissance to the Enlightenment

The secularization of science from the Renaissance to the Enlightenment is a process to which one can put an artificial beginning with Nicholas of Cusa's *De Docta Ignorantia* of 1440, and end with Immanuel Kant's *Kritik der reinen Vernunft* of 1781, which links the Enlightenment to Romanticism. Modern secularization, beginning as a political movement, scored its first success with the *Golden Bull* of 1356, in the empire of Charles IV, the culmination of a tradition that inspired Luis of Bavaria in his struggles against John XXII, following the theories of Marsilio of Padua or William of Ockham. The movement was to reach its apogee after the limit of the present study, with Feuerbach's *Das Wesen des Christentums* of 1841 and Nietzsche's *Also sprach Zarathrustra* of 1883. I propose to concentrate on the period between Pius VI (1447-59), the first humanist pope, and Pius VI (1775-99), the pope at the time of the French Revolution. This period is essential for an understanding of the "death of God" question that is so much at the forefront of modern theological speculation.[1]

---

[1] Cf. A. Auer, "Säkularisierung," in *LTK* IX (1964), p. 253; C. Ratschow, "Säkularismus," in *RGG* V (1961), pp. 1288-96; A. Dondeyne, "Sécularisation et foi," in *Lumen Vitae* 3 (1968), pp. 415-30; A. Durand, "Sécularisation et sens de Dieu," in *Lumière et Vie* 89 (1968), pp. 61ff.; F. Gogarten, *Verhängnis und Hollnung der Neuzeit. Die Säkularisierung als theologisches Problem* (Stuttgart, 1953); A. Auer, "Gestaltwandel des

I
SECULARISM OR CHRISTIANITY: A FALSE ALTERNATIVE

It is impossible to talk of the secularization of science without being clear as to the meaning of the term. Pierre Duhem rightly said that the Fathers of the Church, "in the name of Christian doctrine, opposed the pagan philosophers on matters that we would now consider more metaphysical than physical, but which formed the cornerstone of classical physics".[2] In fact, it was first the biblical theologians, and then the apologists and the Fathers themselves, who criticized the basic thought patterns

---

christlichen Weltverständnisses," in *Gott in Welt, Festgabe für K. Rahner* I (Freiburg, 1964), pp. 338-65; J. B. Metz, "Weltverständnis im Glauben, Christliche Orientierung in der Weltlichkeit der Welt heute," in *Geist und Leben 35* (1962), pp. 172ff.; F. K. Schumann, *Zur Ueberwindung des Säkularismus in der Wissenschaft* (Munich, 1950); E. Cassirer, *Individuum und Kosmos in der Philosophie des Renaissance* (Berlin, 1927); idem, *Das Erkenntnisproblem in der Philosophie und Wissenschaft der neueren Zeit* (Berlin, 1920); W. Dilthey, *Weltanschauung und Analyse des Menschen seit Renaissance und Reformation* (Berlin, 1914); A. D. White, *A History of the Warfare of Science with Theology in Christendom* (New York, 1896); G. Bachelard, *Le nouvel esprit scientifique* (Paris, 1941); S. van Mierlo, *La science, la raison et la foi* (Paris, 1948); J. Daujat, *Physique moderne et philosophie traditionelle* (Tournai, 1958); A. Rich, *Die Weltlichkeit des Glaubens* (Stuttgart, 1966). A. Maier, *An der Grenzen von Scholastik und Naturwissenschaft. Studien zur Naturphilosophie des 14. Jahrhundert* (Essen, 1943); C. Michalski, *La physique nouvelle et les différents courants philosophiques au XIVᵉ siècle* (Cracow, 1928); R. Guardini, *Das Ende der Neuzeit* (Würzburg, 1950); D. De Lagarde, *La naissance de l'esprit laïque au déclin du moyen âge* (Louvain, 1962). To this should be added various histories of the Church (Fliche-Martin, Lorca-Garcia Villoslada, Bihlmeyer-Tuechle, etc.) and histories of science (Lain-Entralgo-Lopez Pinero, Mieli, Taton, etc.).

[2] "Au nom de la doctrine chrétienne, les Pères de l'Eglise frappent les philosophies païennes en des points que nous jugeons, aujourd'hui, plus métaphysiques que physiques, mais où se trouvent les pierres d'angle de la Physique antique": P. Duhem, *Le système du monde, Histoire des doctrines cosmologiques de Platon à Copernic* II (Paris, 1914), p. 408. Cf. G. Ebeling, "Die nicht-religiöse Interpretation biblischer Begriffe," in *ZThK 52* (1955), pp. 296-360.

or ethico-mythical nucleus [3] of Greco-Roman culture in the light of the basic patterns of Judaeo-Christian thought. The doctrine of creation, the denial that events on earth were dictated by the stars, the destruction of belief in the eternal return and the disappearance of the classical Pantheon opened up a new world for the Christian, a world *created,* in contradiction of the adage that "everything is full of gods".[4]

This collision, cultural as well as doctrinal, between Judaeo-Christianity and Hellenism in the 2nd century, also produced a secularization, an *Entgottlichung* (de-divinization), of the cosmos, a genuine a-theization of the divine world of the Greeks and Romans, which led to Christians being justly accused of being atheists in regard to the ancestral gods. This demythologization opened up a new world in astronomy and physics, and a new world to the sciences,[5] which had not previously achieved a sufficient degree of independence from theology, nor a consistency which would enable science to be practiced outside a framework of Christianity.

In metaphysical terms, to consider the world as *created* was not yet an adequate springboard for the new science. A radical sort of "making mundane", desacralizing or profaning had to take place for the cosmos to be considered on the basis of its physical makeup. It is one thing to see the world as not-God and created, but still thinkable only in terms of faith, theology and the theocentric structures of Christianity; it is quite another to see a world existing before one's eyes, absolute [6] and autonomous when considered in terms of its physical structure, on the basis of its essence.

For modern man the question of whether the world is created

---

[3] On the "noyau éthico-mythique d'une culture" cf. P. Ricoeur, *Histoire et vérité* (Paris, ²1955), pp. 274-88; C. Tresmontant, *La métaphysique du Christianisme et la naissance de la philosophie chrétienne* (Paris, 1961), pp. 9-85.

[4] *Fragmento A 22* and *A 1* (Diels-Kranz, 1964), pp. 79 and 68.

[5] "Sciences" here means both natural sciences and sciences of the mind.

[6] Absolute is the metaphysical condition of unbased notes. "Absolute, then, is self-sufficient. . . . Essences are in the line of the formation of the

or not is of little interest (this would be to study its contingent metaphysical condition); he wants to learn about the very structures of the world, on the basis of an examination of them in themselves. If this absolute consideration inclines toward pantheism, atheism or deism, this is not secularization of science but *secularism;* recourse to the foundation, to the God of Israel or of Christianity, is not permitted.

In any form, consideration of the non-divine and now profane world is something quite new in history. Man had never before faced the cosmos with the assumption that it rested on nothing other than its own structures, which were to be described scientifically, independently from theology. The world seen as absolute is a product of evolution of ideas about God and about nature, an evolution which, as history shows us, has passed from secularization to militant secularism. Science was to become the chief instrument of this mode of confronting reality. It was not to be mainly the metaphysical approach that was most concerned with the original and final foundation of the world, nor the theological; only science, particularly mathematics (as Niccolo Tartaglia, 1499-1577, saw), would enable man to penetrate the confused secrets of his world. As science advanced, so theology recovered its healthy transcendence over cultural patterns.

The Church, or rather many theologians and the more influential schools, gradually fell into the following opposing scheme of ideas:

DIAGRAM 1

| Science ←————————versus————————→ Christianity |
| (Secularism)   (Christendom) |

Whenever a scientist of the new school discovered an unknown element in the makeup of the cosmos, there followed an im-

---

ultimate foundations on which the whole world, with its [archaic] physical principles, rests": A. Zubiri, *Sobre la esencia* (Madrid, 1963), pp. 208-09.

mediate conflict with the tradition of Latin-Western culture. I shall examine the cases of Galileo and Richard Simon in due course. Copernicus, encouraged by Clement VII in his youth when he published the *Commentariolus* (1530 ?), only avoided condemnation for the *De revolutionibus orbium coelestium* (1543) through the astute intervention of Andreas Osiander, who put his ideas forward as mere "hypotheses". The work was in any case condemned in 1616 as being contrary to the Bible.

The Church was in fact in a difficult situation. On the one side a whole scientific culture was in the air, largely originating in Rome itself; on the other, the results of its investigations were not accepted. Why this apparent contradiction? It arose through a confusion between the supra-cultural values of faith and the cultural values of a particular culture—the Latin-Mediterranean culture of medieval Christendom. *Christendom,* in both its Byzantine and Latin forms, arose in the 4th century after thte triumph of Constantine. It took many of the cultural values of the Greco-Roman world at face value—those based on the Bible and tradition which had withstood the criticisms of the Fathers. But it failed to notice that those traditions, even those based on the Bible, formed a whole cultural conditioning which, though necessary, was not the only one possible. Thus along with the language came a whole host of astronomical, ethnological, physical, geographical, medical, historical, psychological and political hypotheses that, difficult to disengage from the general background, came to constitute the cultural *a priori,* the basic *idée reçu,*[7] of Christendom.

II

THE CORRECT ALTERNATIVE

The great scientific discoveries of the Renaissance and the Enlightenment were to produce a crisis, a great barrage of crit-

---

[7] "Ist die Lebenswelt als solche nicht das Allerbekannteste, das in allem menschlichen Leben immer schon Selbstverständliche, in ihrer

icism directed against the cultural bases of Christendom. These basic cultural values had grown through the thousand years of Mesopotamian and Egyptian civilization, on which the world of the Bible was nourished; they spread along the Mediterranean through Greek civilization in the East and Roman civilization in the West, and consequently through Europe with the Latinization that followed the Roman conquests. Christianity evangelized this world and, without realizing it, became confused with it at a certain cultural level.

The new science, starting with the demythologization begun by the Fathers, questioned certain principles that had come to be "considered" as of faith. Examples of these were: the astronomical descriptions of the Bible, with the earth as the center of the universe and a spherical structure for the heavens; the belief that Moses was the direct author of the law; the acceptance of the demonaical origin of sickness; the direct creation by God of each star and each species of animal; the miraculous appearance of comets in the sky. The new discoveries made the suppositions of old schemes that conflicted with them no longer tenable.

For some churchmen, this was tantamount to questioning the very principles of faith: the world of Christian faith, essentially *trans*cultural, had become united and confused with the values of *a* culture—that of Latin Christendom. Hence there resulted an antinomy that should never have been: science versus Christianity. It should rather have been posited in the following terms:

Typik immer schon durch Erfahrung uns vertraut?": E. Husserl, *Die Krisis der europäischen Wissenschaften* (Haag, 1962), p. 126.

DIAGRAM 2

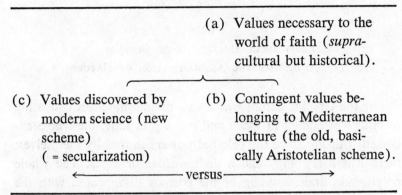

(a) Values necessary to the world of faith (*supra*-cultural but historical).

(c) Values discovered by modern science (new scheme) (= secularization)

(b) Contingent values belonging to Mediterranean culture (the old, basically Aristotelian scheme).

←——————— versus ———————→

Theology and Christianity should have realized that the conclusions could not be in opposition to the values necessary to faith. Yet many theologians, and the most influential ones, held that such discoveries cast doubt on the whole of Christianity. They had mistakenly brought together the (a) and (b) of Diagram 2. Science became tinged with an air of lack of faith, heresy or just plain error. This was not merely a Catholic phenomenon: in the Copernicus-Galileo case, for example, Luther and Calvin took the same attitude as the Inquisition.

The scientists, for their part, who were nearly all originally churchmen, found themselves forced into one of two inevitable errors: either to fall into "concordism"—twisting the Bible or tradition to make it fit in with their scientific conclusions, or to turn from secularization into secularism, setting themselves up against the Church, or at least against many of its theologians. This lack of understanding produced a scientific world which at first grew alongside the Church, but then gradually grew away from it, seeking the autonomy it needed but which was denied it. Modern science was only opposed to the old patterns of Latin culture. Christendom pushed it into secularism. But science itself contained its own impetus toward a new concept of nature and, correspondingly, of God. The general lines along which this impetus evolved will show us the metaphysical basis of modern secularism.

III
FROM SECULARIZATION TO SECULARISM:
THE AUTONOMY AND ABSOLUTIZATION OF NATURE

For the Greeks, nature was a vast divine organism consisting of bodies extending in space and moving in time, the whole endowed with life since the celestial powers moved by themselves; there was a teleology and a divine order or *logos*. The whole polytheistic understanding of the cosmos disappeared with the patristic era and the Middle Ages, but only to be replaced by the angelology and demonology we see reflected in the paintings and other manifestations of medieval culture. Humanism and the Renaissance imposed another pattern. Nature gradually began to take on the pattern of a machine (*natura naturata*) which functions by virtue of certain fixed laws laid down by nature itself (*natura naturans*). This change naturally did not come about overnight, but took centuries.[8]

Flight from the Turks brought the Byzantine sage Plethon (1355-1452) to Italy, where in 1440 he wrote his famous "On the Differences between the Philosophies of Plato and Aristotle",[9] which was to be the spark that set off many a blazing dispute. His disciple Bessarion (1395-1472) defended him in his *De natura et arte*.[10] About this time the young Nicholas of Cusa (1401-64) was sent to Constantinople. The immense evil and refined science of the Byzantine civilization of the time brought about a deep conversion in him. *De docta ignorantia* was the fruit of his morose contemplation of this civilization. His system

[8] R. Collingwood, *The Idea of Nature* (Oxford, 1945); A. Whitehead, *Science and the Modern World* (Cambridge, 1927); E. Burtt, *The Metaphysical Foundations of Modern Physical Science* (New York, 1932); E. Cassirer, *op. cit.;* K. Loewith, *Der Weltbegriff der neuzeitlichen Philosophie* (Heidelberg, 1960).

[9] *PG* CLX, cols. 889-934.

[10] Rome, 1469.

was clearly inspired by the neo-Platonists. Although he asserted the creation of the universe *ex nihilo,* one can already see the birth of the modern tradition: "The world is like a book written by the finger of God." [11] The universe is the *maximum contracto* of everything that is possible, the *explicatio Dei* that pre-existed in God as *complicatio.* This was not yet an absolute view of the universe,[12] but Cusa does abandon Aristotelian cosmology. The earth is no longer the center of the system; the center is now God in all things; the earth is of the same substance as the spheres and could be seen shining like a star if we could get out of "the region of fire" [13] to look back at it. Marsilio Ficino himself (1433-1499) affirmed: "Deus per esse suum quod est simplicissimum quoddam rerum centrum a quo reliqua tamquam lineas deducuntur." [14]

It was the achievement of Nicholas Copernicus (1473-1543) to apply this new view of nature to astronomy. This lay not so much in having dethroned the earth from its central position as in having denied that the universe had a center. Studying our own system, the sun can be considered as its center, but the whole system is made of the same matter and the same astronomical laws govern all parts of the cosmos. The earth is a star just like any other. The whole universe is a vast machine whose structure can be worked out by mathematics. Thus Johann Kepler (1571-1630) could say: "Ubi materia, ibi geometria." Giordano Bruno (1545-1600), even more than Nicholas of Cusa, propounded a neo-Platonic and Renaissance view of nature: God is the *fons emanationis* rather than the creator; "productio rei" is a better term than "creatio". As an enthusias-

[11] "Est enim mundus quasi liber digito Dei scriptus": *Serm. 10;* cf. *Opera* (Basel, 1565).

[12] "Est enim Deus quidditas absoluta mundi seu universi; universum vero est ipsa quidditas contracta": *D. ign.* II, p. 4.

[13] "Si quis foret extra regionem ignis, terra ista in circunferentia regionis per medium ignis lucida stella appareret, sicut nobis, qui sumus circa circunferentiam regionis solis, sol lucidissimus apparet": *ibid.,* p. 12.

[14] *Theol. plat.* II, p. 6; cf. H. Blumenberg, *Die kopernikanische Wende* (Frankfurt, 1965).

tic follower of Copernicus, he held that there is an active divine force present in nature (*natura naturans*) and also in the world as *complicatio explicationis* (*natura naturata*).[15] On February 17, 1600 he was burned alive in Rome, condemned by the Inquisition.

It was with Galileo Galilei (1564-1642) that the new view of nature received its first classical scientific expression: "Philosophy has been written in this immense book which is continually open before our eyes (I am referring to the universe), but which cannot be understood without first knowing the language and recognizing the signs with which it is written. It is written in the language of mathematics and its characters are triangles, circles and other geometric figures, without which it is impossible for me to have a human understanding of these words, and without which I would be wandering vaguely in a dark maze."[16] And he ends by saying that all this has been done "for the benefit of us, Catholics".[17]

Nature is pure quantity, and on these grounds Galileo criticizes and discounts the existence of qualities.[18] This nature, inert matter, must however suppose some cause outside itself. But this cause will henceforth be a *Deus ex machina*. Descartes (1596-1650) pushed this view of the world as a vast machine of matter still further.

[15] "Omnia in uno, omnia in omnibus, unus et omnia, unus in omnibus." "Natura est sempiterna et individua essentia": *Acrotismus Camoeracensis; De Natura.*

[16] "La filosofia è scritta in questo grandissimo libro che continuamente ci sta aperto innanzi a gli occhi (io dico l'universo), ma non si può intendere se prima non s'impara a intender la lingua, e conoscer i caratteri, ne'quali è scritto. Egli è scritto in lingua matematica, e i caratteri, ne'quali è scritto. Egli è scritto in lingua matematica, e i caratteri son triangoli, cerchi, ed altre figure geometriche, senza i quali mezi è impossibile a intenderne unanamente parola; senza questi è un aggirarsi vanamente per un oscuro laberinto": "Il Saggiatore," in *Le opere di Galileo Galilei* VI (Florence, 1933), p. 232.

[17] ". . . per beneficio di noi Cattolici": *ibid.*, p. 233.

[18] ". . . ch'ella [la materia] debba essere bianca o rossa, amara o dolce, sonora o muta . . . non sento farmi forza alla mente di doverla apprendere a cotali condizioni necessariamente accompagnata. . . . Non siano altro che puri nomi"; "Annichilate tutte queste qualità." Cf. G. Galli, *L'idea di materia e di scienza fisica da Talete a Galileo* (Turin, 1963).

It was Baruch Spinoza (1632-1677) who had the courage to give the definitive expression to the idea of nature that began to emerge in the 14th century and that was to make secularism possible. Science claimed that the world was absolute and autonomous in regard to theology. Spinoza formalized this by saying: "By self-causing I understand that whose essence includes its existence." [19] God is his own cause, the only substance, *natura naturans* and *naturata*. Nature is God himself, the expression of his attributes and modes. In this the Dutch Jewish philosopher summed up the whole of the nominalist, humanist and Renaissance tradition of the 16th and 17th centuries. Science now contemplates the universe as pure extent and movement, an absolute that can be worked out by mathematics.[20] This is an absolute immanentism containing its own idealism: *Deus sive natura*.

In England, meanwhile, Bacon had formulated the experimental scientific method. But Isaac Newton (1642-1727) typifies the Anglo-Saxon scientific approach. Nature is a total phenomenom,[21] organized in absolute time[22] and in absolute space;[23] it is the *sensorium Dei* set in motion by absolute movement.[24]

Through idealism, following the Cartesian tradition but also that of Berkeley ("Esse est percipi") and English empiricism, Immanuel Kant (1724-1804) conceived nature as the object (*Gegenstand*) of scientific knowledge. Newton's absolute space and time become the *a priori* of understanding, ordering the

[19] "Per causam sui intelligo id, cuius essentia involvit existentiam": *Ethica* I, def. 1.

[20] "Totam naturam unum esse Individuum, cuius partes, hoc est omnia corpora, infinitis modis variant, absque ulla totius Individui mutatione": *ibid*. II, prop. 13, lemma 7, sch.

[21] "Philosophiae naturalis id revera principium est, et officium, et finis, *ut ex phaenomenis,* sine fictis hypothesibus, arguamus": *Optices* III, q. 28/.

[22] "Tempus absolutum, verum et mathematicum": *Principia Mathematica,* def. VIII, sch.

[23] "Spatium absolutum . . .": *ibid*.

[24] "Motus absolutus est translatio corporis de loco absoluto in locum absolutum": *ibid*.

chaotic world of the *noúmenon:* nature is a phenomenon. Nature
is thought by the *a priori* forms of understanding and cannot be
understood metaphysically, but only scientifically,[25] whereas
things in themselves, neither God nor the "I" on its ontological
level, can be known scientifically. Nature is a transcendental
absolute which has ended by losing its own reality. We are now
very far from the spheres of the 13th century, but very close to
the crisis of modern science. The idealist mechanism of this view
was to be criticized by the vitalist- and biologist-inspired philosophies of the later 19th century.

Goethe expressed the enthusiasm of modern man when he
exclaimed: "Nature! She surrounds us and embraces us, incap-
able as we are of escaping from her, and unable as we are to
penetrate her more deeply. Without our asking or noticing, she
catches us up in the cycle of her dance and carries us with her
until we fall back exhausted into her arms again." [26]

IV
PANTHEISM, DEISM AND ATHEISM

As we have seen, the idea of an absolute nature always and
logically posits a certain idea of God, a God who gradually fades
away until he has practically disappeared from view, in the vi-
sions of Holbach, Feuerbach and Nietzsche.[27]

---

[25] Cf. *Kritik der reinen Vernunft: Transzendentale Elementarlehre* (A
19, B 33) and *Die transzendentale Logik* (A 50, B 74).

[26] "Natur! Wir sind von ihr umgeben und umschlugen unvermögend,
aus ihr herauszutreten, und unvermögend, tiefer in si hineinzukommen.
Ungebeten und ungewarnt nimmt sie uns in den Krieslauft ihres Tanzes
auf und treibt sich mit uns fort, bis wir ermüdet sind und ihrem Arme
entfallen": *Die Natur,* fragment, 1782: *Naturwissenschaftliche Schriften*
I (Leipzig, Inselverlag), p. 9.

[27] Cf. W. Scholz, *Der Gott der neuzeitlichen Metaphysik* (Pfullingen,
1957); C. Fabro, *Introduzione all'ateismo moderno* (Rome, 1964); *idem,*
"Genesi storica dell'ateismo contemporaneo," in *L'ateismo contemporaneo* (Turin, 1968), pp. 3-54: "Questa dissoluzione dell'idealismo
nell'ateismo avviene in due tappe: prima l'assunzione del panteismo di

From the thinkers of the 14th century up to Campanella (1568-1639), the idea of God always resembles either the first *ousía* of the neo-Platonists, the God of Duns Scotus or that of Meister Eckhart, the first moment preceding all emanations, always with a hidden leaning toward pantheism. In the great mechanist systems, God is the organizing architect, the origin of movement and the end of all matter. Copernicus, Kepler and Galileo all see him in this way. Descartes himself makes this idea of God the key to his whole system. But in this new scheme it is in fact an *idea* of God that carries out the function of subjectivity. It is no longer the living, transcendent, provident God of Israel. It is a *Deus ex machina,* put there for the convenience, viability and rational and mathematical understanding of the theoretical structure of modern science and idealist subjectivity. This tradition culminates in Spinoza's philosophical fusion of God and nature. Nature here becomes definitely all; the rest is nothing. The creator and provider has been displaced, but before reaching the stage of declared atheism God was reduced to the idea of a being—a supreme being, admittedly—in the variant known as deism.

In France it was Pierre Bayle (1647-1706) who initiated the process.[28] All the dogmas of positive religion had to submit themselves for examination before the tribunal of reason.[29] In *Pensées diverses sur la comète qui parut en 1680* (1683), his aim was to show that there was no connection between science and revealed religion. He proves that the comet (Haley's) which was seen in December 1680 had no miraculous or providential origin, that it was not an indication of the wrath of God, but

Spinoza da parte di Lessing (*lo Spinozastreit*) e poi l'elevazione dell'Io kantiano ad Assoluto nell'idealismo (*lo Atheismusstreit*) di Fichte" (p. 14).

[28] Cf. B. Magnino, *Illuminismo e Cristianismo* (Brescia, 1959); P. Hazard, *La crise de la conscience européenne* (Paris, 1935); Preclin-Jarry, "Les luttes politiques et doctrinales aux XVIIe et XVIIIe siècles," in Fliche-Martin, *Hist. de l'Egl.*, t. XIX, 1 (1955).

[29] *Réponse aux questions d'un provincial*, cap. CXXVIII.

simply a natural astronomic happening. His god is not a god of providence; miracles are impossible. He goes on to make the first apologia for atheism in Western culture.[30]

In England Lord Herbert of Cherbury (1582-1648) first sketched out the deism that was to receive its fullest expression with Hobbes (1588-1679). The Earl of Shaftesbury (1671-1713) made a distinction between the theism of believers (including Christians) and the deism of those who preach or accept only a natural religion. He had already criticized positive religion in *An Inquiry Concerning Virtue or Merit* (1699), in which he propounded a natural autonomous morality independent of any revealed religion. The moral philosophy of Hutcheson, Adam Smith, Diderot and even Herder and Kant was to owe much to him.

In his *Christianity not mysterious* (1696) John Toland (1670-1722) paved the way for the religious skepticism of Hume (1711-1776), who in his *Dialogues Concerning Natural Religion* (1751-55) denies revealed religion and provides the bases of the natural religion of the philosophers of the French Revolution. Denying the God of revealed religion became constantly more acceptable, particularly with the initial shocks provided by the developing sciences of history and philology. The Bible appeared to have little chance of standing up to the attacks made on it by the new sciences of the mind.

The deism expressed by Diderot in the *Encyclopédie* (1751) turned into a naturalist pantheism, which Baron Holbach (1723-1789) used in his *Le système de la nature* (1770) to set out the first frankly materialist modern concept of nature. He attacks the God of natural religion as well as the God of revealed religion, and his atheism leads directly to that of Feuerbach: "O nature, sovereign of all beings! And you her adorable daughters: virtue,

---

[30] "Que ce qui nous persuade que l'athéisme est le plus abominable état ou l'on se puisse trouver, n'est qu'un faux préjugé que l'on se forme touchant les lumières de la conscience, que l'on s'imagine être la regle de nos actions, faute de bien examiner les veritables ressorts qui nous font agir": *Pensés diverses*, n. 233.

reason, truth! Be our only divinities forever; it is to you that the incense and praises of earth are due. Show us then, O nature, what man must do to obtain the happiness you make him desire? . . . Reason! Lead his uncertain steps on the ways of life. . . ." [31]

This is the replacement of God by nature, pure matter. Modern man, having gone through the nominalist and Renaissance neo-Platonist phases, is defined by Descartes as *cogito*. For the thinking consciousness the world and God fade away as *ideas*. It is a process of anthropology taking the place of everything else. For Kant the world is representation (*Vorstellung*) organized by the transcendental "I". Things (*tà ónta*) and God have vanished from the horizon of the knowable. Only objects systematically organized as nature remain. The subject constitutes himself originating subjectivity; *man is the measure of all things.*[32] This is now the situation of secularism.

V

GALILEO'S PROPHETIC VIEW

From the Renaissance to the Enlightenment, science produced a complete, autonomous and absolute view of the world, independent of theology or revelation. Why did this happen? There are many factors to account for it, but not the least important was the attitude taken by the Church in conflicts whose repercussions were certainly resounding at the time. Having taken the option of our Diagram 1, science *versus* Christianity, it made the process of secularization into a secularism. Science, which

---

[31] "O nature! Souveraine de tous êtres! et vous ses filles adorables, vertu, raison, vérité; soyez à jamais nos seules divinités, c'est-à-vous que son dûs l'encens et les hommages de la terre. Montre-nous donc, O nature! ce que l'homme doit faire pour obtenir le bonheur que tu lui fais désirer. . . . Raison! conduis ses pas incertains dans les routes de la vie. . . .": *Le Système* II, ch. XIV.

[32] Protagoras, *Fragment B 1* (Diels-Kranz II, p. 263). It is clear that the sophist's text has no idealist sense.

was a fruit of the Church's age-long attempt at demythologizing the world, turned against its progenitor, whereas it should have been the Church itself that encouraged secularization, not as absolutization but as the due autonomy of political, economic, cultural and scientific life, of a civilization come of age.

As it is impossible in this article to follow all the conflicts between the Church and science step by step, let us take some prototypical examples. The age of humanism and the Renaissance admired achievements in the realms of geography, astronomy and physics; the age of the Enlightenment discovered history, philology and other sciences of the mind, which presented Christianity with even greater problems.

It is easy today to show the contributions made by many churchmen to the development of science. There are the Humanists such as Marsilio Ficino, Pico della Mirandola, Lefèbre d'Etaples, Erasmus, Luis Vives, Thomas More and so many others. What concerns us here is rather the process of secularization itself, the slowly growing autonomy of the sciences from theology and the Church; the *conflicts* created show the particular reactions of two ways of consciously being Christian—Diagram 1 for some, and Diagram 2 intuitively adopted to a sufficient degree by others, unfortunately not in positions of sufficient authority within the institutional Church.

Christopher Columbus' voyages were based on the fact that the earth was round. This hypothesis was accepted as possible by the theologians of Salamanca and La Rábida. Magellan first sailed round the world in 1519. Therefore the geographical description in Psalm 104 had to be set aside. Is the earth then a star like the other stars in the sky? Geography posed questions of astronomy. Copernicus proposed the sun as center of the system. Tycho Brahe (1546-1601) opposed this "hypothesis". It was only with Galileo, who possessed a great capacity for expressing himself and for theorizing, as well as great theological intuition, that the conflict became public, universal, and immediate. From 1610 to his death in 1642, one of the clearest examples of the secularization of science was acted out.[33] When he was forty-six he published *Sidereus nuntius magna longeque mirabilia spectacula pandens*. In a letter of May 12, 1612 he wrote that his discoveries "were the funeral rites, or rather the end and last judgment of pseudo-philosophy. . . . What will they of the Peripatos not say in order to defend the immutability of the heavens".[34] Note that for Galileo his opponents were the defenders of the "old scheme" (cf Diagram 2). For our purposes the letter he sent to one of his disciples, the Benedictine monk Castelli, on December 21, 1613, is vital. It was later to be the cause of his delation to the Roman Inquisition and the Congregation of the Index by Frs. Caccini and Lorini, O.P. This letter shows that for Galileo the Sacred Scriptures cannot err in any way,[35] but their interpreters can be mistaken.[36] Galileo, firm in his Catholic orthodoxy, regarded the Scriptures and nature as the works of God, who cannot contradict himself.[37]

He set out his thought with greater length, clarity and precision in the letter he wrote to Christine de Lorraine in 1615. He

[33] Cf. M. Virgano, "Fede e scienza in Galileo," in *La Civiltà Cattolica* 116 (1965): I, pp. 33-45; 228-39; II, pp. 35-47; 447-55; A. Dubarle, "Les principes exégétiques et théologiques de Galilée concernant la science de la nature," in *Rech. Sc. Ph. et Th.* I (1966), pp. 67-87; A. Koyré, *Galilé et la révolution scientifique du XVIIᵉ siècle* (Paris, 1955); G. Di Santillana, *The Crime of Galileo* (Chicago, 1955); Gemelli et al., *Nel terzo centenario della morte di Galileo Galilei* (Milan, 1942); J. Yela Utrilla, "Galileo el ortodoxo," in *Rev. Fil.* 1 (1942), pp. 99-125; J. Ortega y Gasset, "Ideas en torno a las generaciones decisivas en la evolución del pensamiento europeo," in *Obras completas* V (Madrid), pp. 9-164.

[34] ". . . la quale novità dubito che voglia essere il funerale o più tosto l'estremo et ultimo giuditio della pseudofilosofia . . . e sto aspettando di sentir scaturire gran cose dal Peripato per mantenimento della immutabilità de i celi": Letter to the Count of Sesi, May 12, 1612, in *Le Opere* XI, p. 296.

[35] ". . . non poter mai la Scrittura Sacra mentire o errari": Letter to Benedetto Castelli from Florence, December 21, 1613, in *Le Opere* V, p. 282.

[36] "Se bene la Scrittura non può errare, potrebbe nondimeno talvolta errare alcuno de'suoi interpreti ed espositori . . . quando volessero fermarse sempre nel puro significato delle parole . . . è necessario che i saggi espositori produchino i veri sensi": *ibid.*

[37] ". . . perchè, procedendo di pari dal Verbo divino la Scrittura Sacra e la natura, quella come dettatura dello Spirito Santo. . . .": *ibid.*

repeats his fundamental principle that the Scriptures cannot lie to us;[38] they contain certain principles of faith (*de fide*) which are beyond man's natural comprehension, and science can have nothing to say about these; they have to be received with faith in revelation. But the Scriptures also contain natural truths, some of which cannot at the present time be proved either way (such as, for example, the question of whether there is life on the stars); some, on the other hand, have been proved with indisputable evidence.[40] In these latter cases, if there is some apparent contradiction between science and the texts of Scripture, then the real meaning of the scriptural passage must be studied carefully, without haste, making the doubtful texts conform with others that are clearer.[41] Galileo inevitably falls into "concordism", but despite this his sure Christian faith and feeling of solidarity with the Church are quite apparent.

He adds that the Scriptures contain some principles which are of faith, but others which are only put forward to make revelation intelligible to a particular culture, such as the Hebrew.[42] Every culture contains patterns which are obvious to it, accepted by general opinion and social consensus.[43] These patterns are dif-

---

[38] Non poter mai la Sacra Scrittura mentire": Letter to Madame Cristina de Lorena, Grand Duchess of Tuscany, in 1615: *Le Opere* V, p. 315. Cf. F. Russo, "Lettre de Galilée à Christine de Lorraine," in *Rev. Hist. Soc.* 17 (1964), pp. 330-66.

[39] "Io non dubito punto che dove gli umani discorsi non possono arrivare, e che di esse per consequenza non può avere scienza, ma solamente opinione e fede, piamente convenga conformarsi assolutamente col puro senso della Scrittura": *ibid.*, p. 330.

[40] "Indubitata certezza": *ibid.*

[41] ". . . concordi col fatto dimostrata. . . . Concordare un luogo della Scrittura con una proposizione naturale demostrata": *ibid.*, pp. 330-31.

[42] "Che dunque fosse necessario attribuire al Sole il moto, e la quiete alla Terra, per non confonder la poca capacità del vulgo e renderlo renitentee contumace nel prestar fede a gli articoli principali e che sono assolutamente *de Fide*": *ibid.*, p. 333.

[43] "Ma più durò, che non solamente il rispetto dell'incapacità del vulgo, ma la *corrente opinione* di quei tempi, fece che gli scrittori sacri nelle cose non necessarie alla beatitudine più si accommodorno all'uso ricevuto che alla essenza del fato. . . . L'assenso de gli uomini tutti, concordi nell'istesso parere, senza che si sentisse la contradizione di alcuno": *ibid.*, pp. 333-36.

ferent from those described by science, but necessary for the understanding and expression of revelation. "But the mobility or stillness of the earth or the sun are not [principles] of faith." [44] The Fathers of the Church appear to be opposed to the astronomical principles recently discovered, but in reality this is only because they did not examine the question seriously or scientifically. Their unanimity on the subject has no force in the scientific field, in which Christians of the new age to which Galileo belongs are doing what the Fathers were unable to do.[45]

It can be seen that Galileo had a perfectly developed Christian understanding of the questions of his age, as well as a theological intuition perhaps surprising in one untrained in the subject. He opted automatically for the right alternative in overcoming the crisis between Christianity and science by showing the transcultural dimension of faith while rigorously opposing the "old system". If this path had been followed, the passage from Christendom to a Christianity understood and expressed within the new modern cultural framework would have been achieved without struggles, misunderstandings and, worse, the alienation of the Church from the world of science.

Without Galileo being able to defend his thesis before the Tribunal of the Inquisition, the doctrine of heliocentrism and the movement of the earth was condemned as "senseless, philosophically absurd, and formally heretical" on February 24, 1616. Two days later, Bellarmine told Galileo the verdict. Bellarmine, for his part, had written a fairly revealing letter to Foscarini on April 12, 1615, in which he said that if Galileo had defended the principle of heliocentrism as Copernicus had done, hypothetically,[46] saying that it was presumed that the

[44] "Ma la mobilità o stabilità della Terra o del Sole non son *de Fide* nè contro a i costumi [Galileo is clearly referring to the decisions of Trent], nè vi è chi voglia scontoro luoghi della Scrittura per contrariare a la Santa Chiesa o i Patri": *ibid.*, p. 337.

[45] ". . . che tal particolar disquisizione non si trova esse stata fatta da i Padri antichi, potrà esser fatta da i sapienti della nostra età, li quali, ascoltate prima l'esperienze, l'osservazioni, la ragioni e le dimostrazioni, de'filosofi ed astronomi": *ibid.*, p. 388.

[46] "*Ex suppositione* e non assolutamente": Letter of Robert Bellar-

earth moved,[47] but without claiming that this *really* happened,[48] there would be no trouble. To claim the reality of such a doctrine seemed to him highly dangerous, since it attacked philosophy, theology, and Sacred Scripture.[49] Bellarmine, as can be seen, identifies faith—(a) in our Diagram 2—with cultural frameworks—(b) in the same Diagram. He lives in an integral and indivisible framework of Christianity.

This is clear from the fact that he argues that Galileo's hypotheses call into question everything that has been said by the Greek and Latin authors on the subject.[50] What they would have done was throw doubt on and show the lack of foundation of many of the cultural systems of the Mesopotamian and Mediterranean worlds, cultural beliefs that had been held for forty centuries. Bellarmine could not accept that any element of these could be questioned, thereby in some sense confusing faith with a particular culture. This led him to propose a distinction by which the entire cultural baggage of primitive Hebrew-Christian culture would become *de fide:* "It cannot be said that this [the matter under debate] in not a question of faith, because even if it is not a matter of faith *ex parte obiecti,* it is a matter of faith *ex parte dicentis."* [51] As a result whatever is written in the Bible becomes, word for word, literal truth for all men of all cultures. Bellarmine leaves no place for secularization, and so, without realizing it, launches science on the road of secularism.

---

mine to Paolo Fascorini from Rome, April 12, 1615: *Le opere di Galileo* XII, p. 171.

[47] "Che supposto che la terra si muova et il sole stia fermo si salvano tutte l'apparenze . . . e questo basta al mathematico": *ibid.*

[48] "Ma volere affermare che realmente il sole stia nel centro del mondo . . .": *ibid.*

[49] "E cosa molto pericolosa non solo d'irritare tutti i filosofi e theologi scholastici, ma anco di nuocere alla Sacra Fede con rendere false le Scritture Sante": *ibid.*

[50] ". . . et a tutti li espositori greci et latini": *ibid.,* p. 17.

[51] "Nèsi può rispondere che questa non sia materia di fede, perchè se non è materia di fede *ex parte obiecti,* è materia di fede *ex parte dicentis":* ibid.

He himself was not particularly interested in the value of the sciences in themselves. He was waiting for a proof of the centrality of the sun or the movement of the earth from arguments drawn from Scripture alone, and so he could exclaim: "They have not proved it to me." [52] Therefore the subsequent course of events should not surprise us. For decades and decades Catholic theologians went on maintaining that the earth was the center of the solar system.

VI
THE APPEARANCE OF PHILOLOGY

The Bible, which means the very bases of faith, also seemed to be under attack at a much deeper level. As early as 1506 the leading Hebrew scholar of his day, Johann Reuchlin (1455-1522) had published his *Rudimenta linguae hebraicae,* and *De Verbo mirifico* had appeared even earlier, in 1496. For pointing out numerous mistranslations in the Vulgate he was condemned by the Inquisition of Mainz in 1513, a condemnation approved by the universities of Cologne, Louvain, Mainz and Paris in 1514, and finally by Leo X himself in 1520. But it was to be in France, considerably later, in the days of Bossuet (1627-1704), Louis Quatorze and the Edict of Nantes, that this debate was to come to a head with really serious repercussions.[53] The chronological discoveries of scientific historical investigation and the advances made in the study of the history of language could not leave the Bible on one side. In the West Indies, the studies of the Inca

---

[52] "Ma io non crederò che ci sia tal dimostratione, fin che non mi sia mostrata": *ibid.*

[53] Cf. P. Hazard, *op. cit.;* G. Schnueer, *Katholische Kirche und Kultur im 18. Jahrhundert* (Paderborn, 1941); W. Dilthey, *Friedrich der Grosse und die Aufklärung, Gesam. Schriften* II (1921); E. Cassirer, *Die Philosophie der Aufklärung* (Tübingen, 1932); E. Guyenot, *L'évolution de la pensée scientifique, les sciences et la vie aux XVIIe et XVIIIe siècles* (Paris, 1941); Latreille-Palenque, *Histoire du catholicisme en France* II-III (Paris, 1962).

civilization made by Josè de Acosta had showed how narrow the views of universal history based solely on a European viewpoint were, while Saint-Evremond in his *Réflexions sur les divers génies du peuple romain* first questioned the mythical accounts of the origins of Greece and Rome. Romulus was reduced to a mythological figure. But Bossuet objected to this hypothesis which questioned the established patterns of Mediterranean culture, and so of Christianity: "The first age shows you in the beginning a great spectacle: God creates the heavens and the earth by his word (year 1 of the world; 4004 B.C.)." [54] Then scientific chronology showed, with Paul Berzon in his *L'antiquité des temps rétablie* (1687), that the Egyptian dynasties began before the dates assigned to the flood, and continued without interruption.

Now it was the turn of the "past" to start moving, the earth, thanks to Galileo, having lost its immobility some time before. More serious was the appearance of the philological works of Richard Simon (1638-1712), a Catholic priest of the Oratory and a loyal son of the Church to his death, with sharp and penetrating intelligence, fantastic memory and unshakable tenacity. Studying in the Oratory, this early philologist was able to consult Hebrew manuscripts of the Bible. [55]

He knew Greek, Hebrew, Syriac and Arabic well and was a tireless reader of the Fathers, particularly of Jerome, from whom no doubt he received his combative spirit. His first work shows his knowledge of the tradition of the Eastern Church. [56] Shortly before, he had defended the Jewish community of Metz

[54] "La première époque vous présente d'abord un grand spectacle; Dieu qui crée la ciel et la terre par sa parole (an du monde 1; dev. J. C. 4004) . . .": "Histoire Universelle," in *Oeuvres complètes de Bossuet* X (Paris, 1866), col. 687.

[55] *Ms. hebreo 1295,* Bibliot. Nat. Paris. Cf. F. Strummer, *Die Bedeutung Richard Simon für die Pentateuchkritik* (Münster, 1912); R. de la Broise, *Bossuet et la Bible* (Paris, 1891); A. Monod, "La controverse de Bossuet et de Richard Simon au sujet de la version de Trévoux," in *Cahiers Rev. Hist. et Phil. Rel.* (1922); A. Molien, "Richard Simon," in *DTC* XIV (1941), pp. 2094-2118.

[56] *Gabrielis metropolitae Philadelphiensis* . . . (Paris, 1671).

against a false charge of murder, in a spirit that we would now call ecumenical.[57] He tried to undertake a joint translation of the Bible with Protestants, which earned him the following reproach from Bossuet: "Ten years ago, a group of gentlemen from Charenton resolved to embark on a new translation of Scripture; Justel, a Protestant whose learning is well known, proposed to Simon that he join the project; Simon himself drew up the plan of this new version; all together jointly decided to give the public a French translation *that would not favor any side* and that would be equally useful to Catholics and Protestants alike. . . . Doubtless [he adds ironically] this is a fine undertaking for a Catholic priest!" [58] So Simon, perhaps, is the forgotten founder, without immediate followers, of Catholic ecumenism.

Simon wrote many other works of an ecumenical tenor.[59] Finally there appeared his major work, *Histoire critique du Vieux Testament* (Paris, 1678). The aim of the whole argument is apologetic: the Bible is "not sufficiently clear in itself to establish the truth of faith independent from tradition".[60] Simon shows that the texts have a long and complex history from the scribes and prophets to his own day: "Des revolutions du texte hebreu de Moïse jusqu'a nos jours." God did not speak Hebrew to Adam; Moses is not the sole author of the Pentateuch; the Samaritan Pentateuch can be authentic; Esdras must have been one of those principally responsible for the composition of the Bible as we have it; the Septuagint introduces important variations, and so does the Vulgate.

All his criticism is opposed to the rationalism of Spinoza and the anti-traditionalism of Luther and Calvin. Simon's aim is to defend orthodoxy and so he extends infallible inspiration to

[57] *Factum servant de réponse au livre intitulé: Abrégé du procès fait aux juifs de Metz* (Paris, 1670).

[58] *Critiques de la version du N.T.* VI; *Oeuvres complètes* X, col. 604.

[59] *Cérémonies et coutumes des juifs* (Paris, 1674); *Voyage du Mont Liban traduit de l'italien* (Paris, 1675); *Factum contre les bénédictins de Fécamp* (Paris, 1675).

[60] ". . . claire d'elle-même et suffisante pour établir seule la vérité de la foi et indépendente de la tradition": *Preface.*

the authors, scribes, compilers and composers of the Bible.[61] What happened was that Protestants, Jansenists and Catholics in general, starting with Bossuet, were scandalized by his use of the new philology, by this sort of secularization of the Bible through making it the object of scientific investigation. At the instigation of Bossuet, the police, by order of the Conseil du Roi, withdrew the 1,300 copies that had been printed from the market. A few got through to London and Amsterdam, and were passed avidly from hand to hand.

Simon produced several other exegetical works.[62] He wrote: "He who seeks to see truths of physics, mathematics, astrology, or any other part of philosophy (sic) in certain passages of the Scriptures, which do not treat of these matters except in passing and in terms common among the [Hebrew] people, is committing an act unworthy of a theologian and a philosopher." [63]

[61] "Le Saint-Esprit les a conduits d'une manière qu'ils ne sont jamais trompès dans ce qu'ils ont écrit": Prologue to *Lettre à M. l'Abbé P. touchant l'inspiration des Livres sacrés* (Rotterdam, 1699).

[62] Among the more important are: *Novorum Bibliorum polyglottorum synopsis* (Utrecht, 1684); *Histoire critique du texte du N.T.* (Rotterdam, 1689); *Histoire critique des versions du N.T.* (Rotterdam, 1690); particularly *Histoire critique des principaux commentateurs du N.T. depuis le commencement du christianisme* (Rotterdam, 1693). Here Simon says: 'Il es difficile de tirer des conclusions de l'Ecriture, comme d'un principe clair et évident" (p. 94). Bossuet regards this as a disqualification of Scripture: (". . . pour montrer qu'on ne gagne rien avec l'Ecriture": *Defense de la tradition et des Saints Pères* II, 1; *Oeuvres complètes de Bossuet* X, p. 175), but he fails to see that Simon is only indicating the difficulties posed by philology and history, which cannot be avoided in biblical studies. He was still to write *Le Nouveau Test. de J.C. traduit sur l'ancienne édition Latine* (Trévoux, 1702), in which he states: "Notre version Latine érant obscure et équivoque en quelques endroits, il n'y a point d'autre remède pour être ces obscurités que d'avoir recours aux originaux. . . . Ce n'est pas que je blâme ceux qui publient des réflexions morales sur l'Ecriture, mais je souhaiterais qu'elles fussent toujours jointes à des interprétations littérales" (*Preface*); and finally, *Moyens de réunir les protestants à l'Eglise romaine* (Paris, 1703).

[63] "Celui qui voudrait établir les vérités de la physique, des mathématiques, de l'astrologie, et de toute autre partie de la philosophie, sur de certains passages de l'Ecriture, qui n'en font mention qu'en passant et en des termes usités parmi le peuple, ferait une chose indigne et d'un théologien et d'un philosophe": *Bibliothèque critique* IV (Basle, 1710), p. 96.

Simon distinguished clearly (cf. Diagram 2) between the cultural, changeable patterns of the Bible and transcultural faith. As a scientist and philologist he overthrew many cultural patterns in order to demonstrate the universal transcendence of faith. Bossuet, on the other hand, as a Defender of Christendom, failed to make this basic distinction. A letter to him written by Capperonnier in 1702 tells him that before criticizing Simon he has to have a very good knowledge of the science of philology. Bossuet has failed to observe this rule and so has been led into important errors.[64] Bossuet thought that Simon's literary criticism overthrew the whole of theology and tradition.[65] He confused tradition with a "traditionalist" exegesis, and this is why, when Simon showed that the Fathers did not possess sufficient equipment to discover the full meaning of the texts from the Hebrew version, he exclaimed that Simon had the "dark design to destroy the bases of religion".[66] In his view, the science of philology invalidated the Bible.[67] By a decree of December 1, 1682, Simon's main work was placed on the Index, where most of his other works were, and were to remain until this instrument went into its last edition.

[64] "Comme M. Simon veut triompher en fait de grec et d'hebreu . . . il faut apporter un grande exactitude . . . cette importante règle n'a point été observée [par vous même]": *Oeuvres* XI, col. 1077.

[65] "Selon ce critique, on ne doit suivre que les règles de la grammaire, et non pas la théologie de la tradition, pour bien expliquer le Nouveau Testament. Si l'on fait autrement, ce n'est pas le sens de saint Paul que l'on donne; c'est celui que l'on s'est formé sur ses propres prejugés": "Lettre CCX de M. Arnauld," July 1693, in *Oeuvres complètes de Bossuet* XI, col. 1066. Arnauld expresses Bossuet's thought precisely, with an unthinking opposition between science (philology) and traditional theology (i.e., that of Christendom).

[66] ". . . un sourd dessein de saper les fondements de la religion": Letter to Nicole, December 7, 1691, in *Oeuvres* XI, col. 998. But it cannot be denied that Simon sometimes went too far. Cf. H. de Lubac, *Histoire et Esprit* (Paris, 1950), pp. 425-26.

[67] "Et l'on va voir que le résultat est précisément ce que j'ai dit, que l'Ecriture et ensuite la tradition, ne prouvent rien de part et d'autre": *Défense de la tradition* II, 1; *Oeuvres* X, col. 172.

VII

CONCLUSIONS

History is mistress of life because she shows that what happened in the past goes on happening in the present. Bossuet in this dispute took the same position as Bellarmine in the Galileo crisis. He confused, in fact if not in design, the necessary patterns of faith with certain relative patterns of a particular culture. The critical viewpoint of science, from the Renaissance to the Enlightenment, and far more afterward, required a differentiation between faith, the essential, and cultural patterns. Modern science displaced many mythical expressions—the centrality and immobility of the earth, the Hebrew or Roman chronologies, etc. And yet the great institutions rejected the astronomy of Galileo, the philology of Richard Simon, the geography of de Clave, Bitaud and Villon (condemned by the Sorbonne), the chemistry that from the time of Paracelsus (1493-1561) was suspect because confused with alchemy and magic, Priestley (by the Anglicans), the first doctors (either on account of disection or vaccination—Boyer condemned by the Sorbonne), and many, many more. . . . Their rejection could not help but transform a healthy secularization into an anti-Christian secularism. At the very least it was one of the causes of this, and not a minor one. Christendom was protected for a time by the efforts of some of its protagonists such as Bossuet, but the price paid was a further opening of the gates of incredulity, indifference and secularism in the Europe of the 18th century. Montesquieu, Voltaire, Rousseau and the French Revolution could have been a positive movement instead of one of anti-Catholic secularism. The Church failed to welcome science wholeheartedly as a daughter, and only did so jealously and against its will. The false antinomy science-Christendom prevented a growth to maturity. Only those who recognized the supracultural transcendence of faith in the very rout of the "old system" achieved a dispassionate understanding of the positive value of secularization. This secularization-become-secularism now presents us with a culture *etsi Deus non daretur.*

Joseph Comblin/*Recife, Brazil*

Secularization: Myths and Real Issues

Over the past ten years something has changed in the relationship between the Catholic Church and the world. But what exactly is it that has changed? Is it the real relationship between Church and world that has changed, or simply our own conception of this relationship? At present the theory of secularization is being urged upon us with great vigor, but we cannot help being a bit distrustful about it. Does secularization represent a theory, a new myth, or an embodiment of the real facts?

If we want to judge the changing conditions of the present in the light of the Gospel, we must make a preliminary distinction between two different questions: (1) What does the Gospel have to say about what is really happening today between the Church and the world? (2) What does the Gospel have to say about our way of conceptualizing what is taking place?

Some feel that there has been no important change in the

relationship between the Church and the world. As they see it, only our conceptions of this relationship have changed; we now view our relationship with the world in a different way. Our new Christian conception, however, is just as false and one-sided as the older view was; it is the by-product of our present ideologies. Despite the varying ideologies that are around, the Church continues to march along her old route and to remain faithful to her basic ways of operating.

These people can present a strong argument for their case. They point out that the old institutions are still around, for all the discussion going on. They may have adopted new names, but they are still doing what they were wont to do before the debate started. Specifically, it is still the same people who are making the fundamental decisions. We now say "the laity" instead of "the flock", "dialogue" instead of "apostolate", "compromise" instead of "obedience" and "serving the world" instead of "conquering the world for Christ". But we continue to do exactly the same things. At the moment of truth we find that nothing has really changed.

Others feel that we have simply changed our tactics within an overall strategy that ever remains the same. Since the time of Leo XIII, the Church has come to realize that she could no longer count on her traditional alliances to ensure the continuing existence of her institutions in human society. Therefore she has made an effort to attract the support and sympathy of the new social classes, hoping thereby to find new allies and new instruments for carrying out her policies in the world. She has adopted certain "democratic" forms to win the support of the lower classes, the support of the lower middle class in particular. Catholic Action represented one stage in this tactical evolution, and conciliar dialogue represented another stage. All the rest is mere theory or rationalization.

I personally think that more than that is actually taking place. But I would not go so far as to say that the theory of secularization is a faithful reflection of what is actually happening.

Some would have us believe that at present the Church is coming around to acknowledge and accept the phenomenon of secularization. This, they say, is the profound happening in the present day. Such an interpretation must be examined critically. We would readily admit that the theory is quite successful at winning converts; its ability to convince people is one of the signs of the times. But this success is not proof of its correctness. We must try to find out what the real situation is.

I
BEFORE THE COUNCIL

To measure the profound change that has taken place in our conception of the Church-world relationship, we need only read the older social encyclicals—up to the *Summi Pontificatus* of Pius XII. In them we continually find an idealized image of medieval Christendom, spawned from the imagination of romantics (Novalis), and the notion that this Christendom is disintegrating more and more under the daring attacks of Satan. It is an assault that begins with the Protestant Reformation and continues in present-day atheism (de Maistre, de Bonald, Balmes). Our current history is the continuation of a fall that was provoked by Luther.

In his inaugural encyclical, Pius XII pointed out that the Church had given spiritual cohesion to Europe. Educated and civilized by the cross, Europe was then able to teach other nations and other continents. Once our separated brothers detached themselves from the Church's infallible magisterium, however, many of them ended up by rejecting the central dogma of Christianity: the divinity of Christ. In this way they accelerated the trend toward spiritual dissolution. In short, the welfare and happiness of human society depends upon its recognition of the pope's infallible magisterium. Once this fundamental bedrock is rejected, nothing can stop the irreversible decline toward misfortune and eventual ruin. Already society was at such a level of degradation that only the blind could fail to see the horrible finale. As Pius XII put it: "The anguish and trouble of the present day are the most convincing argument for Christianity that one could ask for."

In *Divini Redemptoris,* Pius XI had proceeded from this same notion of spiritual decline. The struggle between good and evil, our heritage from original sin, continues to plague the world. The ancient tempter continues to deceive the human race with his false promises. That is why confusion and disruption has gone on century and century, to reach its high point in the contemporary age. Revolution threatens to break out everywhere, surpassing all the prior persecutions of the Church in scope and violence. Whole nations are on the verge of falling back into a barbarism that outdoes the savagery which reigned when the Savior came to earth. The barbarism today is atheistic communism, which seeks to overthrow the social order and to undermine the foundations of Christian civilization.

In this conception of reality, the world itself is passive. It is the prize in an age-old battle between Satan and the Church. The danger is now acute, because Satan has piled up an impressive string of victories. In destroying the Church, which created Western civilization and maintained the social order, Satan is leading the world toward destruction. Is it not apparent that this whole conception more faithfully mirrors the categories of Greco-Roman political philosophy than the Christian lineaments of the New Testament? The antithesis between civilization (order) and barbarism is part of the Greco-Roman conception. Changing the terms somewhat, these encyclicals pose the same objections to the modern world that Celsius posed to the first Christians.

In the pre-conciliar days of the 20th century, the popes accepted secularization as an unfortunate but indubitable fact. It was the result of the errors which Satan had inspired in heretical Christianity and modern philosophy. The work of the Church, consequently, was to wage war against these forces of destruction in the hope of restoring the medieval order.

In the 19th century, by contrast, the Church's struggle had been viewed more as an heroic defensive action. The Church would stand firm against assault, winning by the weight of her inertia (Lacordaire). With the rise of Catholic Action in the early days of the 20th century, the Church was already thinking in terms of reconquest. Her task would be to restore the social order of Christ the King. Even Maritain's notion of replacing sacral Christianity with a profane Christianity did not radically alter this perspective. The Church's task was to "consecrate the world to Christ", rendering it obedient to his sovereignty.

The only thing that would change would be the means to this end. No longer would the Church seek to reestablish a Holy Empire of neo-Catholic nations. Now it was felt that reconquest could be achieved through democracy. Yet all during this period the world was seen as inert matter waiting to be shaped and ordered by Christian forces. History was still seen as a process of decline and restoration, with Christianity the only positive, active force.

II
AFTER THE COUNCIL

After the Council, a new orientation became evident and new theories were proposed, but some lines of continuity remained and there was no complete break with the past. The new outlook was present while the Council was in preparation, and the old outlook is still defended by a minority. It is the relative strength of each viewpoint that has changed.

Today Christian thought starts out by recognizing the world's inherent values and dynamisms. It is not just a piece of inert matter that is destined to receive its shape and form from the Church. In according inherent value to the world, some go so far as to see in it an "implicit" (Schillebeeckx) or "anonymous" (Rahner) Christianity. No longer are we to conquer the world; now we are to dialogue with it. Instead of asserting her rights against the world, the Church now acknowledges her servant role to the world.

In according autonomy, freedom and pluralism to the world, we introduce the notion of the diaspora (Rahner). Scattered throughout the world, Christians are present to other men as witnesses and explainers of Christ. The process of de-Christianization is now given a favorable interpretation: it marks the end of the Counter-Reformation, the Constantinian epoch and the established Church. We are urged to see the good points in atheism and communism. These are the predominant themes in our new conception of the Church-world relationship.

Many go further and frame these themes in a general theory of secularization. Even when they do not do this, the influence of this theory can be seen in their presentation of the themes already mentioned. That is why I feel compelled to ask about the validity of this theory. Does it hold up as an interpretation of the changes which are taking place today in the Church-world relationship?

It is interesting to see how the great idealist philosophical systems of the early 19th century continue to dominate our conceptions of the world. When Harvey Cox describes secularization as the advent of a pragmatic age that will succeed religious and metaphysical thinking, he is merely repeating Comte's law of the three stages. When he follows Gogarten in asserting that secularization places in man's own hands the responsibility of forging human values, we recognize the voice of Fichte and Hegel. Does the secularization theory represent anything but traditional Christianity's late discovery of the alluring idealist philosophies and the end of Thomistic censure over Christian thought?

As A. J. Nijk remarks,[1] little has been added to the secularization theory of Gogarten. It is to the latter that we must return
if we want to pass judgment on the value of this interpretative
theory. Up to Gogarten's time, secularization was viewed as a
movement unfavorable to Christianity. From his time on, people
began to view secularization in a more favorable light. What
exactly did all this represent: a new discovery or a process of
mystification?

To some extent it certainly did involve mystification. Gogarten's "Copernican revolution" was based on an identification between faith and idealist principles that we must regard as
suspect. He identified the three attributes of an authentic dialectical faith with three fundamental theses of Fichte's and
Hegel's idealist philosophies. In this way the Christianity of
Barth and Bonhoeffer came to be identified with that of Hegel.

To begin with, Gogarten asks us to follow Luther, as rein-
terpreted by Barth and Bonhoeffer. We are to recognize that
authentic Christianity is: (1) faith without religion (i.e., without
a religious "experience" or pietism); (2) the weakness of God
(i.e., without Christianity or any establishment); (3) the world-
liness of the world (i.e., *Weltlichkeit* without clericalism and
sacralization). This authentic Christianity is to be identified
with three constituent elements of idealism: (1) demythologization; (2) the advent of the kingdom of the Spirit without
any law; (3) the historicization of man, who creates his own
destiny. In short, Gogarten sets up the following equation:
religion + Christianity + sacralization equals myth + legalism + an
absence of history. Consequently, faith equals idealism equals
secularization. The word "secularization" describes both the
movement of history as described by the idealist philosophers
and the formation of an authentic faith.

Once one has set up this conception of history, he is easily
tempted to find verification of it in the real situation. Today the
aid of religious sociology is invoked in the attempt. People isolate facts that point toward de-Christianization and then assert

[1] See A. J. Nijk, *Secularisatie* (Rotterdam, 1968), p. 71.

that they are truly representative of our epoch. Such facts would be the decline of religious practice and ecclesiastical influence in certain sectors of modern society.

To complete the theory, people link up the above with the explanation offered by certan sociologists for the so-called process of de-Christianization—i.e., the formation of an urban, industrial society. So, in its final form, the equation is this: Secularization equals authentic faith equals idealism equals de-Christianization equals an urban, industrial society.

III
WHAT HAS CHANGED IN THE WORLD?

If the real situation does correspond to this theory, then we can understand people's optimism in the present situation. The same facts, which a few years earlier epitomized the sad state of the Church and the imminent collapse of the world, now are optimistic and hopeful signs of a better future. If the theory is right, then the Church's forward march is synchronized with the forward march of history; we are at one with the hour of history. Secularization represents a great opportunity for Christianity, and de-Christianization is a comforting phenomenon.

One might well ask whether this nice theory was not spawned to give us some assurance and certitude in an age of uncertainty and transition. To begin with, certain fundamental objections come immediately to our mind. When it expects the advent of authentic Christianity to come from the time of history, it is relying on the suspect eschatology of Joachim of Fiore (c. 1145-1202). Moreover, in charging history with the task of reforming the Church, it dispenses Christians from the difficult and perduring task of fighting against the sins of their institutions. Finally, in proclaiming the advent of a "post-Christian" age, it leaves little or no room for an ecclesiastical institution. Does the reality conform to this theory? Does Christian revelation corroborate it? Our changed attitudes are supposedly inspired by changes in the world, but what exactly has changed in the world?

People tell us that we are participating in a new phenomenon, the historicization of man. It involves, on the one hand, desacralization, and, on the other hand, the advent of man as his self-creator. Here we must join Audet [2] in denouncing these new and false versions of the myth of Prometheus. People are simply handing us a myth if they present de-sacralization as the struggle of profane reality to emancipate itself from the sacred—as if the primitive world had been totally immersed in the sacred, and history represented the profane world's continuing attempt to wrest reality from the clutches of the sacred. In reality, the world has never been totally sacralized; and there is no evidence that we can ever have a totally de-sacralized world. Likewise, we have never had a totally primitive, sacral mentality, and we probably shall never have a totally rational, unsacral mentality.

I do not see any way in which industrialization and urbanization could produce a total change from complete sacralization to no sacralization at all. The fact is that today, as at other critical turning points in civilization, we are witnessing a displacement of sacred and profane realities. The sacred is changing its proper point of relevance and application, but there is no hard evidence that it will disappear. The Bible, to be sure, does show us that revelation involves some process of de-sacralization vis-à-vis the other contemporary religions of the Near East. Specifically, it involves the de-magnifying of nature, politics and morality. But the Bible does not present human history as a gradual transition from total sacralization to total de-sacralization. On the contrary, man from the very beginning is both secular and religious at the same time.

[2] See J. P. Audet, "La revanche de Prométhée," in *Revue biblique* 73 (1966), pp. 5-29.

Our real problem is to discover the forms of sacral life that are shaping a new civilization. The same thing holds true for man the creator. The new technologies of our day do not represent something that is totally and absolutely new. We do not start with a totally passive human race and struggle gradually toward an active mankind. We do not start from total heteronomy and gradually move toward total autonomy. From the day of creation on, we find a thread of continuity in the development of man. He did not have to fight for autonomy, for he had it from the start.

As far as demythologization is concerned, people are handing us a myth when they try to say that man's primitive mentality was totally mythic. Man has always mixed myth and science, and he will continue to do so. The boundaries are being changed. Myth disappears here, to reappear there. The Bible does not eliminate the mythic element entirely. It establishes a certain relationship between the ineffable God and mythic expression. Its language represents demythologization vis-à-vis certain kinds of language, but it can easily represent a new mythologization vis-à-vis other kinds of language.

Finally, let us consider the denunciation of moral legalism and the appeal to the freedom of the Spirit that has been orchestrated so magnificently by such figures as Nietzsche, Marx and Freud. As some would have it, their work does not allow us to think ingenuously anymore; we must now examine everything with a critical eye. But the fact is that their incisive critique is aimed against the Church's function as the guardian of morality and the social order. This is a function which she took on when she entered into the structure of Roman society; her clergy accepted the role of moral mandarins within this society. It is this role, the role of religion in Roman society, that is now untenable; the role lasted so long because the fundamental structures of this society perdured until a very short time ago. But law and the freedom of the spirit will always combine in some sort of relationship, and Christianity has its own peculiar way of conceiving this relationship.

In short, we might well say that two things are taking place in the world right now: (1) a rearranging of the frontiers between the sacred-mythic and the profane-scientific, prompted by the new urban, industrial society; (2) the demise of Roman society and the role which religion played in it.

As far as de-Christianization is concerned, I should like to see some hard proof of secularization. The facts are certainly open to debate, and American sociologists generally dispute the data that point toward de-Christianization. The comparisons made between present faith and practice and that of other ages is instructive. For example, it does not seem that sacramental attendance in the Middle Ages was one whit superior to sacramental attendance today. Here, too, we find variations and fluctuations, but we do not find a gradual transition from Church adherence to non-adherence. The Churches, whose death knell was sounded long ago, seem to be surviving pretty well.

III
WHAT HAS CHANGED IN THE CHURCH?

What has really changed in the Church? Are we really moving toward a "faith without religion"? Some forms of piety and religious experience are clearly on the wane. But is it not true that in the new charismatic communities, which some see as the future shape of the Church, we see the rebirth of other forms of pietism, religious experience and mystic feeling? In that which some call "personal" faith, are there not quite a few elements of "religion" alongside "authentic" faith?

Faith is above and beyond religion, but it is not wholly detached from religion. In any case, desacralization itself is not enough to form an authentic faith. Destroying religion will not produce faith. Today as always, real faith is nurtured by the preaching of the Gospel. The mission of evangelizing the world today will not be accomplished simply by secularization. It ever remains the challenge hurled at the apostles.

The death of Christianity and the advent of a totally secular world were announced a long time ago, along with the appearance of a helpless God. But if Christianity is an intermixture of Church and culture, it will continue to exist. It is the Christian conception of the family and education that makes it what it is. Even the old temptation to manipulate and dominate the politics of nations for spiritual ends still exists—only in different forms. Cox rejects the mandarin role of the Church, but he talks about the role of "intellectuals" in an industrial society. Such a role could create new forms of Christianity that would be quite as suspect as the old role.

Finally, the yearning for purity and the notion of an impotent God need not necessarily lead to a diaspora. The Church has always known the temptation to form little communities on the margin of human society. The community churches of today echo the yearnings of the monks in an earlier day. But if Christianity wants to transform the world, it must ever start from its perduring ambiguity and seek to accomplish the challenge laid down to it. Secularization does not solve the problem. The eternal challenge simply takes on new forms.

Let us not interpret the present changes in mythical terms. We are not confronted with the decline of the world, or the birth of a new humanity. One civilization, the Greco-Roman civilization of the past, is disappearing—and with it, the role which religion and the clergy exercised in that civilization. A new urban and industrial civilization is coming to birth, causing a new displacement in the sacred and mythic elements. But there is no reason to enmesh all this in the framework of idealist philosophy. To create a theory of secularization is to echo the old dream of Joachim of Fiore in modern terms. It is to ask that history purify Christianity and perform the task alloted to each new generation of Christians.

The danger of this eschatology is that it gives us a false assurance. Our new-found optimism, a product of this eschatological dream, may well be one of the reasons why post-conciliar spiritual progress has been so poor. Another danger is that this eschatology may discourage pastoral analysis and effort. We feel that history will do the job for us, and we fail to seek ways of involving ourselves in the new society that is taking shape. We lack missionary drive and purpose.

PART II
BIBLIOGRAPHICAL
SURVEY

Irénée-Henri Dalmais, O.P./*Paris, France*

Sacralization and Secularization
in the Eastern Churches

It would appear that up until now the secularization of Christian life and the doubts cast on the sacralization of the Church's institutions and life have not created much stir among Oriental Christians, perhaps because the questions are judged inopportune. It might be better to say that those of them who care to listen to the increasingly strong protests voiced in certain milieus and regions are surprised and ill at ease. There are only a few who, like N. Nissiotis,[1] seem to have some idea of the consequences of a technological civilization for Christian thought. The fact itself that most countries of the Orthodox tradition—in other words, the majority of the Oriental Christians —live in a situation dominated by an officially atheistic ideology seems to strengthen even those who live in the West in their reluctance to take a calm look at this growing secularization.

However, there is more to it than a mere attachment to the ancestral heritage bequeathed by Byzantium and kept alive by a liturgy which impregnates the whole of Christian life in the various traditions of the East. Eastern theologians and thinkers rightly denounce the extreme consequences of the present pro-

[1] "Le sens théologique de la révolution technique et sociale," in *Contacts* 59/60 (1967), p. 232.

tests which they consider as excesses produced by Western Christianity. In theology they think that the importance of natural theology and the treatise on "the one God" (*de Deo uno*) have been stressed at the expense of the Trinity and man's divinization by the gift of the Spirit who inaugurates the new creation and the transfiguring conformation of man to the risen Christ. In ecclesiology they think that attention has far too long, and almost exclusively, concentrated on the Church as a society and on its relations with the secular society.

We shall not deal here with these doctrinal issues but only initiate a discussion and indicate some points which might be pursued in the study of the historical and cultural situations which have considerably contributed to these differences in attitude. While up until now the sacralization of Christianity and the urgency of secularization have found little expression among Eastern Christians, all the signs point to the fact that these issues can no longer be avoided because of the development of a technological civilization and the emergence of the "secular city". It seems likely, and is definitely desirable, that this challenge of attitudes so firmly maintained until now will not be answered by transplanting Western thought but by starting afresh from situations that are essentially those of the Christian East. In what follows we have deliberately left out the vast work already done by Russian thinkers. This would require a study by itself and would be beyond both the scope of this article and my competence. Moreover, little has been done on the historical and cultural lines which I wish to pursue here and to which I shall limit myself.

●

I

THE CULTURAL BACKGROUND AND ITS IMPLICATIONS

Western Christianity is stamped with the indelible mark of the Latin language which for long centuries was the principal and sole official vehicle for its expression. Through this language it is also marked by the culture and the view of the world conveyed by this language. This is particularly relevant for all that touches the "sacred" because for the Romans this concept was a profoundly institutional concept and therefore linked with the organizational structures of society.[2] One recalls Gaius' statement that "only that is considered sacred which has been consecrated by the authority of the Roman people".[3] This is confirmed by the restrictive interpretation of the Word given by Festus in his *De verborum significatione:* "What individuals have dedicated to the divinity for personal religious motives is not considered 'sacred' by the Roman pontiffs." [4] The growing influence of the Eastern religious mentality during the period of the empire never really succeeded in changing this concept which was kept alive by the legal and sacerdotal professions. Whatever the cosmic and therefore divine prestige with which a sacralized empire was gradually endowed, the character of this sacralization always remained above all political, and therefore very different from the divine character of sovereign power in all the Eastern cultures. But it was in these Eastern cultures that the Oriental Churches took root. Research in this complex subject of Oriental Christianity is far less developed than for Latin Christianity, although even here much remains to be done for the clarification of the varied nuances according to the varied cultural milieus where Latin Christianity became established.[5] The heritage bequeathed by the language and culture of classical Greece, although for several centuries the ordinary vehicle for the expression of Chris-

[2] Cf. G. Dumezil, *La religion romaine archaïque* (Paris, 1966), p. 136; H. Fugier, *Recherches sur l'expression du sacré dans la langue latine* (Paris, 1963).

[3] "Sacrum quidem hoc solum existimatur, quod ex auctoritate populi romani consecratum est" (Instit. I, 5).

[4] "Quod autem privati suae religionis causa deo dedicent, id pontifices romanos non existimare sacrum" (424 L. in *Digeste* 1, 8, 6, 3). Cf. the article on "Consecratio," in *Real Lexicon für Antike und Christentum* III, p. 270.

[5] Cf. E. Bartsch, *Die Sachbeschwörungen der römischen Liturgie* 46 (Münster, 1967).

tian thought, are far less important in the Christian East than the Latin language and Roman culture were in the Christian West. Research in these Eastern problems would provide the indispensable basis for a discussion of those issues created by the growing secularization of the human condition, issues which both Eastern and Western Christians have to face.

II
THE HISTORICAL BACKGROUND

It is no less important, particularly in an issue dealing with Church history, to look at the diversity of historical experience which for a large part conditioned the life of the Church in both East and West. The sudden collapse of the empire's institutions in Western Europe in the 5th century, the establishments of Christian kingdoms where for a long time the clergy played an important part in the administration, the exploitation—first by the Frankish kings, then by the Carolingian and Germanic emperors—of the "myth" of David and Solomon whose anointment and consecration became a sacramental rite—all this led the Western Church to that ambiguous regime which is conventionally called "Christendom". The part played by Augustine's *City of God* in trying to provide a doctrinal justification for this regime is well known.[6] Both the historical facts and the ideological constructions to which they gave rise are very different from what happened in the Eastern Churches. At the start we find there the collective experience of a Christian empire which found in the legislation of Justinian both its expression and the principle of its organization. In spite of the vicissitudes of history, the long history of this empire constituted, even for those Churches which claimed autonomy and were most opposed to its unifying pretensions, an exemplar which was never seriously questioned up to our own time. All the Churches worked out their legisla-

[6] H. X. Arquilliere, *L'Augustinisme politique* (Paris, 1934).

tion, with regard to both Church law strictly so called and personal law, within the framework of the Byzantine Nomocanons, incorporating the new rules laid down for the Churches of the Empire.

Typical is the case of the Syro-Oriental Church. Established on the borders of Sassanid Persian Empire, this Church proclaimed in 410 its communion in faith with the "Fathers of the West" and accepted the canons of Nicea. In 424 it claimed complete juridical autonomy, and in 484 it affirmed its unwavering loyalty to the doctrinal tradition of Antioch, of which it considered Nestorius the authentic representative, although he had been removed from office and anatematized by the Churches of the Roman Empire. Yet, this Church, so profoundly individualistic and with an ecclesiology so strikingly similar to that of the Roman tradition, never ceased to be attracted to Constantinople, the spiritual capital of all Eastern Christians.

This common foundation was well and truly laid when the Arab invasion placed the Churches already separated from that of Constantinople, and the sectors of the patriarchates of Alexandria, Antioch and Jerusalem that had remained faithful to the Council of Chalcedon, under a non-Christian rule. The fact that the Byzantine government seemed to be identified with the defense of this orthodoxy was bound to attract those Churches, called Melkite (imperial) for that reason, within the cultural and disciplinary orbit of the Great Church of Constantinople. It would be really useful if the consequences of this process for the way in which the Christian concept of the "sacred" affected the cultural and political order were studied in detail. A study of the Syriac and Arabic versions of the Byzantine liturgical texts which were used until they adopted an almost literal translation of the Byzantine liturgical books, printed at Venice, is still to be made. Speaking more generally, it is the strictly religious vocabulary of the Arabic of the Christians, Orthodox or not, which ought to be analyzed carefully.

From the beginning of the Caliphate, the various Christian

Churches were recognized as "protected communities", and this condition allowed them to preserve a relative cultural autonomy. These communities were now independent of a political authority which—sacred in character because the emperor, being baptized, had a privileged position in the Church—was always liable to interfere. In their function of proclaiming, as Churches, salvation in Jesus Christ, these Christian communities on Islam soil had to assume, as a Church, responsibilities which, on imperial soil, were referred to the civil authority and administration. It is difficult to determine how much the Islamic ideas, which saw all human conduct in the light of the recognition of God's sovereignty and of witnessing to the faith,[7] influenced the ideas inherited from the Christian empire and implied in the very message of the Gospel; did they strengthen or contort them? Whatever the answer, the sacralization of all that human conduct was bound to be seen by the Christians in Islamic lands as the safeguard of their identity and as a witness to their faith with regard to the unbelievers.

With the exception of the Churches in Russia and Ethiopia, almost all the Eastern Christian Churches had to live for several centuries under the domination of Turks converted to Islam. First the Seljuk, then the Ottoman rulers gradually extended the regulations laid down by the Omayyad and Abbasid caliphs to most of the territories once dominated by the cultural and spiritual influence of Byzantium. In fact, the situation was different because, with few exceptions, the Christians of Eastern Europe rarely went over to Islam. The Serbians, Bulgarians, Rumanians and Greeks retained and developed their national awareness, their religion and their language, and these three elements became more closely intertwined as time passed. The role played by the clergy in preserving this national consciousness and later in the emancipation movements that led to independence is not dissimilar to that played by them at the beginning of Western Christendom.

[7] L. Gardet, *La Cité musulmane* (Paris, 1954).

III
A NEW SITUATION

At present it is difficult to see how and in what degree the impact of new conditions and secularizing ideologies imported from outside will give rise to the kind of conflict that is now evident in various Western regions. In spite of their common historical and cultural experience, in spite of the fact that they are at present confronted with an official Marxist ideology, except in Greece, and in spite, also, of their common Orthodox tradition nourished on a Byzantine heritage which so far has not been seriously queried, each of these countries and national Churches shows a situation very different from that prevailing in the various countries of the West which are marked by centuries of Latin Christendom. In spite of its claim, so often asserted, to be the legitimate heiress to the Byzantine legacy and the bulwark of Christian Hellenism, even Greece must find answers today to questions that were never asked in the centuries of the empire. It is unfortunately doubtful whether the majority of those who, either in the ecclesiastical hierarchy or in the universities, are responsible for opening up new ways are in a position to understand the complexity of these questions. Most often, in fact, a total loyalty to the legacy of Orthodoxy as a whole, identified with the inviolable tradition of "Christian Hellenism" understood as the sole authentic interpretation of the apostolic message, as the Fathers understood it, is simply put side by side with a university culture of Western origin. Many and clear indications make one fear that this simple juxtaposition will not be able to stand the strain much longer. The Christians of Greece will soon have to face the problems of secularization, but at the moment no one can see what the reaction will be.

Apparently only some Russian theologians living in the United States have begun to express some views which will make it possible to start the discussion with some clear ideas. First among them is G. Florovsky who on several occasions has stated in what sense and with what distinctions it will be possible to keep the concept of "Christian Hellenism" alive.[8] Two of his disciples, A. Schmemann and J. Meyendorff, have also repeatedly, though discreetly, queried the permanent value of the Byzantine concept of the sacred for Orthodoxy. But this is only a timid beginning. On the other hand, in France two Orthodox laymen, P. Evdokimov and O. Clément, have seriously studied the very conditions of a Christian existence in a secularized world, and the same holds for the Greek theologian N. Nissiotis. The meeting which brought together some Orthodox theologians then staying in Western Europe in May 1967 at Massy, near Paris, showed how little most of them were interested in such problems.[9] This holds still more for those who, in Greece and in the Middle East, not to mention the Popular Democracies, try to preserve intact the heritage of a sacralized Christianity which has not yet faced up to the tensions that have been tearing for a long time at Western Christianity.

The Orthodox, and in general all Eastern Christians, like to stress three points which they think will protect them against the dangers of an extreme secularization which they are anxiously and painfully watching in certain sectors of Western Christianity. They say, first of all, that in the East the Church has always been seen as a communion in the mystery of God's life rather than as an institution governed by legal regulations and an authority in principle similar to that of the temporal powers. As S. Bulgakov has often said, the Church is heaven on earth, mainly because of the sacramental rites. The Church for them is preeminently the liturgical assembly of which the traditional modes of expression, handed down from the Fathers, have never been queried up to the present. Finally, Christian life is the gradual transfiguration

---

[8] Cf. Y. N. Lelouvier, *Perspectives russes sur l'Eglise* (Paris, 1968), p. 127.

[9] Text of the papers read: *Contacts* 59/60 (1967), pp. 3-4.

of mankind and through it of the whole cosmos, in the likeness of the risen Christ. Thus the Eastern Christian tradition, deliberately ignoring on principle the dichotomies of various kinds which have long beset the West, can only be opposed by one other form of secularization, namely that of atheism, and this is radically incompatible with the faith. One cannot have a dialogue with it, one cannot refute it, and all one can do is to oppose it with the peaceful witness of a "life in Christ". Whether this confidence can be shaken by the advent of a technological civilization, a predominantly scientific culture, lay institutions not bound to an anti-Christian ideology, and all the developments which have already been at work for so long in the West, we do not know, and it would appear to be premature to answer this question in any definite sense. It is moreover likely that the situation will develop very differently in the Arab world, where Islam dominates the scene and the problem of secularization differs in many aspects from the way it exists in countries with a Christian tradition, in Greece, or in the Popular Democracies.

But there are at least two fields in which far more coordinated research from various angles is required than has so far been undertaken. There is, first of all, the liturgy which plays such an important role in the life of the Eastern Christians and in their concept of the Church. While it is true that the liturgical traditions of Antioch and Jerusalem have been predominant in all those Churches, it is also certain that not only the ceremonies but also the very understanding of man's relations with God in the liturgical celebrations have been influenced throughout the East by a pre-Christian concept of the "sacred", of which the "imperial cult" of Byzantium is the most obvious expression. Historians of the liturgy [10] and of Byzantine art recognize that there are some outstanding periods, each of which has its own features: the age of Justinian, of the Macedonians, the Comneni and the Paleologues. It is important to find out which "sacred" expressions each one favored. For the rest, and at a more general

[10] H. J. Schulz, *Die byzantinische Liturgie* (Freiburg im Br., 1964).

level, the whole question of "Christian Hellenism" and its relations with Byzantine culture still needs serious study. Without it there is no solid ground for any discussion of the specifically Christian character of the sacred modes of expression to which the Christian East remains so profoundly attached.

[11] C. Delvoye, *L'art byzantin* (Paris, 1968).

Dominique Julia/*Paris, France*
Willem Frijhoff/*Paris, France*

The French Priest in Modern Times

The recent discussions about the social status of the priest invite comment from the historian insofar as he sees the influence of the past on the present situation. The past poses a certain resistance, and it is imbedded in our present whether we are aware of it or not. Determining the exact nature of this resistance from the past is one of the essential spiritual exercises for our time.

How did we manage to get a priest "separated from the world"? How did this radical cleavage manage to last for such a long time? Relying on the help of some recent studies and limiting our comments to the French situation, we would like to attempt to single out some of the contributing influences. Quite obviously, a comparative analysis of the whole European situation would shed a more penetrating light on the whole issue. Considering the present state of research into this question, however, we feel that such an attempt would be difficult to carry out right now.[1]

The Decrees of Trent

The definition of the priest in modern times begins with the decrees of Trent. They are the product of a twofold preoccupa-

[1] P. Pierrard, *Le prêtre français* (Paris, 1969).

147

tion: to give a dogmatic response to Luther's rejection of the sacrament of holy orders [2] and to correct abuses. The dogmatic decree of July 15, 1563 (Session XXIII) puts stress on the sacrificial character of the priesthood. Instituted by Christ, the priesthood's essential mission involves the twofold power of *consecrating* and absolving. The power of preaching was deliberately passed over in silence precisely because the reformationists chose to equate the ministry with preaching alone. Transmitted by a real sacrament (*contra* Luther's assertion that the ceremonies of ordination were a purely human invention), the priestly order helps to give the Church its *hierarchical* structure. In the Church, the spiritual powers always come from above; they are transmitted by Christ, not delegated by the community.

Doctrinally, then, the priest is *superior* to the layman, and this fact determines the nature of their relationship to each other. Nothing is more explicit on this point than the reform decree of September 17, 1562 (Session XXII). It is a logical follow-up to Trent's dogmatic position:

> Nothing does more to instruct men in piety and attract them to pious practices than the life and example of those who have been consecrated to the sacred ministry. Seeing that they have been elevated to a higher order which transcends the things of this world, everyone else looks at them as at a mirror. In priests they find the example which they should imitate. Thus clerics, destined to have the Lord as their portion, should so live and act that their dress, their external demeanor, their bearing, their speech and everything else about them are totally respectable, discreet and religiously appropriate (Chapter I).

Here we find the priestly portrait that would dominate the modern period. First and foremost, the priest is seen as *different*.

[2] A. Duval, "Les données dogmatiques du Concile de Trente," in *Bull. du Comité des Etudes* 38-39 (1962), pp. 448-72.

Berullian Spirituality

In the 17th century, the French spirituality of Cardinal Bérulle followed the doctrinal lead of Trent and centered its thoughts on the priest. The priestly spirituality of the Berullian school, which left its stamp on all 17th-century pastoral reform,[3] follows logically from the priest's union with Jesus Christ, the Word incarnate and the one and only priest-mediator.

"Through the priesthood of Christ, we put on the person of Christ and act in his name and stead." Thus *sanctity* is a necessity for the priest. He must be a priest, not only in the exercise of his powers of consecration and authority, but also "in his person and his interior and exterior life".[4] According to Cardinal Bérulle, passivity and mystical union are the true moral realm of the priest, and he must achieve mystical unity between his function and his way of life.

The priest, a man of prayer, sacrifice and contemplation, is also *superior* to the faithful within an order that is established by God and that is a logical follow-up to the mystery of the incarnation. There is to be a dovetailing between the ecclesiastical hierarchy and the mystical hierarchy of souls:

> In the order established by God, there are two types of people: those who receive and those who communicate Christ's spirit, light and grace. The former are all the faithful; the latter are the priests and superiors, who exert an influence on their inferiors and who themselves must imitate the angels above.[5]

[3] H. Bremond, *Histoire littéraire du sentiment religieux en France* (Paris, ²1967); P. Cochois, *Bérulle et l'Ecole française* (Paris, 1963); J. Choné, "La spiritualité sacerdotale," in *XVIIᵉ Siècle* 62-63 (1964), pp. 112-32; P. Broutin, *La réforme pastorale en France au XVIIᵉ siècle* (Tournai, 1956).

[4] P. de Berulle, "Formulaire des Voeux de servitude à Jésus et Marie," *Oeuvres complètes* (ed. Migne), p. 630.

[5] *Idem*, "Opuscules de piété," *ibid.*, p. 1268.

It is the priest, indeed, who teaches (preaching) and adminis-
ters the sacraments (authority). But he remains, first and foremost, a man of prayer who is predestined to sanctity by his state.[6]
That is why all the spiritual books of that era lay stress on the
eminent *dignity* of the ecclesiastical state, on the quality of his
personal life which should differentiate him from the laity, and
on the external attributes which are to manifest his interior
perfection.

The ideal proposed by the spiritual writers was a reaction
against the uninspiring state of affairs that existed at the start of
the 17th century in France. We need only peruse the *Cahiers de
doléances*[7] to get the picture. We do not know for sure who
wrote these *Cahiers,* but it is apparent that in them the people's
ideals joined forces with a model spirituality. It called for new
dignity on the part of priests who, after the devastating religious
wars, seemed ignorant, dissipated and debauched.

To judge the real effects of the pastoral reform movement, we
must view it on the scale of a whole century. It was certainly
abetted by the hierarchical political structure in which it was
framed. Up to 1789 the clergy remained the first estate of the
realm—a privileged class that enjoyed fiscal and judicial exemptions as well as honorific privileges.[8] Here Trent's view of the
priest as *superior* and *different* found a ready point of impact.
Moreover, once the most crying abuses of the benefice system
(multiple benefices, etc.) were eliminated, the system itself abetted the social integration of the priest. After all, he enjoyed a

[6] In the 17th century pious lay people practiced the priestly virtues.
They, too, performed various prayer exercises, did scriptural reading and
dedicated themselves to the poor. But they were different from the clergy
in that they were not to withdraw from the world. The lay hermitism of
the Port Royal community was regarded as a dangerous menace by the
era from which they retreated. See C. Berthelot du Chesnay, "La spiritualité des laïcs," *XVIIᵉ Siècle* 62-63 (1964), pp. 30-46.

[7] The full title is the *Cahiers de doléances des paroisses du baillage de
Troyes pour les Etats Généraux de 1614,* published by Y. Durand (Paris,
1966).

[8] P. Blet, "L'ordre du clergé au XVIIᵉ siècle," in *Rev. Hist. Egl. de
France* 54 (1968), pp.5-26.

"dignity with ordinary function in the Church, which entitles him to receive revenues".[9]

In the light of recent studies, it seems that the revenue from benefices enabled most priests to live decently, if not luxuriously —contemporary clerical complaints notwithstanding. A society that was wholly Christian in theory agreed to pay its clergy for the eminent services it performed, and these services were still regarded as such by all. Even the *Cahiers de doléances* of 1789 do not radically challenge the social status of the priest; what it deplores is the abusive expropriation of tithes for the benefit of the large religious abbeys.

This spiritual model of the priest saw him as someone set apart from an evil world. It thus involved an "overclericalization" of the priestly state. Priestly culture remained purely theological at the very moment when the overall culture was being laicized and the exact sciences were coming into their own.[10] The effect of this mutation was not fully felt for two centuries. But it is evident that during the 19th century the priest's *difference* came to be regarded as one of *culture* rather than as one of *function*.[11] The sacred, of which the priest was the bearer, received less and less recognition; it gradually came to be regarded as simply the remnant that had not been involved in the progressive secularization of society.

Whether he realized it or not, the priest himself contributed greatly to this outlook by objectifying religious rites and actions. He enshrined them in a clearly defined sacramental setup which excluded everything that escaped his authority: popular festivals,

[9] C. Loyseau, *Du droict des offices*, I, 1; an overall study of clerical revenues and their history is yet to be made. See J. Meuvret, "La situation matérielle des membres du clergé séculier dans la France du XVIIe siècle," in *Rev. Hist. Egl. de France* 54 (1968), pp. 47-68.

[10] A. Degert, *Histoire des séminaires français jusque'à la Révolution* 2 (Paris, 1912); R. Darricau, *La formation des professeurs de séminaires au début du XVIIIe siècle* (Plaisance, 1966); G. Gusdorf, *La révolution galiléenne* (Paris, 1969).

[11] J. Rogé, *Le simple prêtre: sa formation, son expérience* (Tournai, 1965) (covers the period from 1895 to 1939).

pilgrimages, "superstitions", and everything that could give rise
to "abuses" in his estimation. The priest, then, deliberately chose
to restrict the definition of the sacred to certain things. He drew
an *a priori* line between the wheat and the chaff, which may well
have been simply a line between different types or levels of culture: i.e., the urbane, bourgeois culture of the priest [12] vis-à-vis
the culture of the common people.

Throughout the 18th century we find a growing trend toward
moralizing in the vocabulary of the clergy.[13] It is not by chance
that the pastoral visitations of the 18th century repeatedly ask
such questions as these: What are the dominant vices of your
parishioners? What are their good qualities and their shortcom-
ings? An objective moral grid was thus established, which ruled
out analysis of earthly realities from the very start. It became an
abstract law, completely out of touch with human beings and
their preoccupations. This may well account for their growing
disinterest and the eventual phenomenon of "de-Christianization"
about which we know so little.[14]

The French Revolution and its effects are framed in this general context. It served to highlight and harden the existing cleav-
ages. From then on, a *civil* society existed with its own laws and
institutions, and the Catholic religion was simply the religion of
most Frenchmen. The bitter quarrel over *the schools* [15] persisted throughout the 19th century, giving rise to those two im-

[12] Recent studies show that the clergy of the old regime came mostly
from the lower and middle bourgeoisie class. See P. Goubert, *Beauvais
et le Beauvaisis de 1600 à 1730* (Paris, 1960), pp. 198-206; D. Julia,
"Le clergé diocésain du diocèse de Reims à la fin du XVIIIᵉ siècle," in
Rev. Hist. Mod. Contemp. 13 (1966), pp. 195-216.

[13] B. Groethuysen, *Les origines de l'esprit bourgeois en France* I (Paris,
1927).

[14] R. Rémond, "The Problem of Dechristianization," in *Concilium* 7
(1965), pp. 149-57. On the contempt for terrestrial realities, see L.
Perouas, *Le diocèse de la Rochelle de 1648 à 1724* (Paris, 1964).

[15] A. Prost, *Histoire de l'enseignement en France: 1800-1967* (Paris,
1968), pp. 155-222. The problem of instruction being secularized had
arisen in 1762 with the expulsion of the Jesuits: see Caradeuc de la
Chalotais, *Essai d'éducation nationale ou plan d'études pour la jeunesse*
(1763).

placable antagonists: the teacher and the local curate, the anti-clerical and the cleric. Both sides remained entrenched in their respective ideologies, and their debate may well provide us with the best example of the Church's refusal to acknowledge the on-going secularization.

It was the school issue that prompted the multiplication of "independent" schools and the many clerical initiatives to pre-serve and save the few who could be saved from the clutches of a satanic world. It was the typical rearguard action of a fossilized organism, clinging desperately to the structures of a bygone age, to the old Christian social order that was no more.

A New Conception of the Priest

It was not until the years 1890-1900 that a new conception of the priest and his role began to grow. By that time the essential cleavage was no longer between clergy and laity but between Christians and non-Christians. Decisive here were the new ideas set in motion by such movements as *Sillon* and *Démocratie chrétienne*, and by the ecclesiastical Congresses of Reims (1896) and Bourges (1900).[16]

Gradually the notion spread that the priest should "go to the people" and preach a "social religion". Christian Democrats be-gan to broach the idea that the priest should put himself on a level of professional equality with the masses he was trying to evangelize; evangelization was to be effected "from below" and not "from above".[17] As yet we do not find any general notion of worker priests,[18] of course, but there was talk about priests being journalists, lecturers, economists and elected officials.

The democratic approach to evangelization, in which the priest is no longer *superior* to his audience, began to awaken new and

[16] R. Rémond, *Les deux congrès ecclésiastiques de Reims et de Bour-ges: 1896-1900* (Paris, 1964); see J. M. Mayeur, *Un prêtre démocrate: l'abbé Lemire* (Paris-Tournai, 1969).

[17] M. Montuclard, *Conscience religieuse et démocratie* (Paris, 1965), pp. 173-81.

[18] Except in the *Journal d'un prêtre d'après-demain (1902-1903)* of Abbé C. Calippe, reissued by E. Poulat (Paris-Tournai, 1961).

deep desires in the priest. He longed to become a real human being once again, to be reborn a man: "Might we not have a pilgrimage of priests, marching toward their rebaptism as human beings? Might we not discard the shackles of this odious system, where the pastor thinks for the curate, the bishop for the pastor, and the government for the bishop?" [19]

In short, it was the overall status of the Church in society and clerical education as a whole that were called into question during this period. These ideas were not able to bear full fruit at the time, however, because of the climate engendered by the Separation (1905) [20] and the hardening of Rome's position. But the future would be a different story.

The Current Crisis

All these lines of force converged toward the priestly crisis we now face. The 20th century, the century of the laity, is dominated by a fascination with the priest.[21] There is no contradiction here, however, because now the priest holds popular attention primarily as a social paradox. The Church's problem of acculturation is crystallized in him.

Until the present day, the priest was seen as the only qualified interpreter of terrestrial realities. But with the laicization of middle-class culture, he had lost the last vestiges of his social role. Lacking anything to say, he ran the risk of shutting himself up in ritual and facing the "ignominia saeculi" (E. Renan). Such a purely *spiritual* ministry over an objectified sacred could only leave him profoundly dissatisfied. For he now lived in a secularized society where "the well-known formula—'he who works,

[19] Abbé P. Darby, cited by M. Montuclard, *op. cit.*, p. 179.
[20] X. de Chalendar, *Les prêtres au Journal Officiel: 1887-1907* (Paris, 1968).
[21] This matter should not be overstressed. A careful estimate shows that the number of books on the priest has not risen in France between 1959 and 1968 (20 to 25 per year). Since 1964, however, the number of books on the priestly *crisis* has grown, while the word "priesthood" in the titles has gradually given way to the word "priest". Careful study of exact circulation and readership remains to be undertaken.

prays'—finally has meaning".[22] Two series of events had to take place before a *generalized* awareness of this transformation became manifest and helped the priest to move out from his isolation.

First of all, the general situation of the priest changed after the Separation. The drop in vocations alarmed the Church.[23] The loss of revenue gradually led to a rehabilitation of manual labor. The experience of two world wars forced many priests to live their priesthood in an existential, human way, to plumb the depths of the cleavage that existed, and to glimpse the specific values of a secularized world.[24] The existence of widespread non-Christianity became clear to the priest, forcing him to redefine the priestly function in terms of *mission*.[25]

Secondly, the priest witnessed the awakening of the apostolate of the laity and took part in the process.[26] The seeds planted by the social Christianity of an earlier day began to bear fruit. Recognition of the enormous proportions of the religious decline led to the formation of *Catholic Action*. This involved a "total" Christianity, where the process of acquiring personal perfection went beyond ecclesiastical exercises to include the *social* apostolate. Once the laity took cognizance of its own specific mission, once it no longer defined itself in terms of the clergy, then a new definition of their respective relationship became inevitable—and Trent's vision of a Church of clerics came tumbling down.

Thus the priest was driven to an awareness of his professional non-productivity, while at the same time he felt uncertain about his role within the Church. On the other hand, his new experiences demolished his contempt for the world and reanimated his own flagging hopes. He discovered two things: the presence of an *outside world* and the primacy of *lived experience*.

[22] J. Jaures, *La question religieuse et le socialisme* (Paris, 1959), p. 46.
[23] D. Julia, "La crise des vocations: essai d'analyse historique," in *Etudes* (1967), pp. 238-51, 378-96.
[24] E. Poulat, *Naissance des prêtres ouvriers* (Paris-Tournai, 1965).
[25] H. Godin—Y. Daniel, *La France: pays de mission?* (Paris, ⁷1962).
[26] A. Dansette, *Destin du catholicisme français: 1926-1956* (Paris, 1957).

The pressure of sociological phenomena gave rise to a revised plan of pastoral action and new theological reflection in the thirties and forties. There was a gradual transition from ortho-*doxy* to ortho-*praxis*. Apostolic presence took precedence over ritual gesture. The theology of spiritual character gave way to a theology of mission which was ratified by Vatican Council II.[27] Ontological sanctity tended to be replaced by missionary virtues; the latter were conceived not so much in terms of the priest him-self as in terms of *others*. The priest was to convert these others, or to dialogue with them.

The attention of the priest now found a different focus. The notion of a well-rounded cultural background was replaced by the world of work, the latter being viewed as the real locale of lived experience. The priest's material situation continued to change, and he moved toward the ranks of the marginal prole-tariat. The priest of Trent, *teaching* the universal truth of a wholly Christian civilization, was replaced by a priest *living* earthly reality in an emancipated culture in order to discover the truth that comes with experience.

No longer would the priest be *superior* and *different*. The clerical state of earlier centuries had lost its *raison d'être* in a transformed society. The phenomenon of the worker priests [28] represented a radical break with the old Christian social order, for in the latter it was the priest's isolation from the world that guaranteed the authenticity of his message. The *Mission de France* [29] followed the same new line, seeking to get beyond the old, outmoded territorial strictures.

[27] J. Moingt, "Caractère et ministère sacerdotal," *Rech. Sc. Rel.* 56 (1968), pp. 563-90; *Les prêtres: décrets "Presbyterorum ordinis" and "Optatam totius"*, texts and commentaries under the editorship of J. Frisque and Y. Congar (Paris, 1968). The changing titles in each suc-ceeding schema of "Presbyterorum ordinis" are almost a resumé of the history of the priest since Trent. It went from *De clericis* to *De sacerdo-tibus* to *De ministerio et vita presbyterorum*. See R. Wasselynck, *Les prê-tres: élaboration du décret "Presbyterorum ordinis" de Vatican II* (Paris, 1968).

[28] See E. Poulat, *op. cit.*, pp. 15-34, for a critical bibliography.

[29] J. F. Six, *Cheminements de la Mission de France: 1941-1966* (Paris, 1967).

The priest had come to a new outlook. He now judged himself in terms of his "presence to human life and activity". A liberated and liberating message tended to replace the old, rite-bound message. The priest wanted to become a man with a living message to communicate,[30] and a rather ill-informed public opinion did not always keep up with the evolution taking place.[31]

The new orientation is manifested in two ways. First of all, the walls of separation have come tumbling down, as the cassock and the old-style seminarian drop out of sight.[32] Secondly, the whole sacerdotal function is being slowly reshaped. Older, more experienced men are being recruited for the priesthood.[33] A new style of life, more mobile and communitarian, becomes evident.[34] The methods and structures of the apostolate are being revised.[35] The priest is becoming a true professional man.[36] The hope is that all these changes will produce optimum conditions for communication.

Two Fundamental Options Available

It is at this point that we encounter another problem that will always be involved in the question of the priest's status. It is the more general problem of the relationship between the Church and society. Two basic options can be discerned.[37] On the one hand, we might have a *teaching* Church that would integrate her-

[30] M. Bellet, *La peur ou la foi: une analyse du prêtre* (Paris, ⁵1968).

[31] J. Maitre, "Les prêtres vus par l'opinion publique," in *Le clergé français* (Paris, 1967), pp. 227-53; *Les français et le prêtre* (inquiry by Sofres), in a special issue of *La Documentation Catholique* 50 (1968).

[32] G. Artaud, "Le jeune séminariste," in *Vocation* 245 (1969) pp. 7-107.

[33] P. Huot-Pleuroux, "Nouvelles méthodes de recrutement et de formation," in *Le clergé français* (Paris, 1967), pp. 141-225. The summons to adult men was already evident in the missionary situation in China (1667). See the "Mémoire" of F. de Rougemont, in *Anal. Boll.* 23 (1914), pp. 279-93.

[34] A. Manaranche, *Prêtres à la manière des apôtres* (Paris, 1967).

[35] F. Connan—J. C. Barreau, *Demain, la paroisse* (Paris, 1966).

[36] P. Huot-Pleuroux, *La formation permanente du clergé* (Paris, 1969).

[37] F. A. Isambert, "Nouveaux prêtres ou aggiornamento du clergé français," in *Tendances et volontés de la société française* (Paris, 1966), pp. 322-46.

self into present-day society in order to communicate her message. On the other hand, we might have a Church *bearing witness* and taking a stand vis-à-vis a civilization that tends to erase the specificity of the sacred. Thus we would have a trend toward modernization or a trend toward stripping down. A different type of priest would result, depending on which option we choose; we would have a priest who attests, or a priest who contests.

At the same time, a third type of priest is taking shape in a society growing more and more flexible. He sees himself as one who would embody all forms of challenge to the world; while fully acknowledging the reality of the secularized world, he would challenge (and, at the limits, reject) the forms and internal structures of this secularity.

Framed within this conflict of options are the three problems facing the priest today: his professional work, obligatory celibacy, and the structures of authority. It is no accident that these three problems are involved, because work, sexuality and the use of one's critical judgment are three basic constituents of every human life. It is in these areas that people expect to hear a liberating word from the priest, whether it be through his words, his actions, or his simple presence.

The question takes this form: Should "declericalization" [38] be total,[39] or should it stop at some limit defined *in advance* by the priest's role as mediator between the transcendent and the

[38] J. Duquesne, *Demain: une Eglise sans prêtres?* (Paris, 1968); I. Illich, "Métamorphose du clergé," in *Esprit* 35 (1967), pp. 584-601; B. Lagrange, *Un autre prêtre* (Paris, 1968) (picks up the articles of M. Oraison in *Le Monde*, April 9-10, 1968). For a Marxist approach see A. Casanova, "Le Concile et le malaise des prêtres," in *La Nouv. Critique* 12 (1968) pp. 15-22. On professional work, see A. Monjardet, *Autre prêtre, autre Eglise* (Paris, 1967); E. R. Wickham—J. Rowe, *Mission industrielle ou prêtres ouvriers?* (Paris, 1967) (originally in English, this book well illustrates the conflicting options available). On celibacy: M. Oraison, *Le célibat: aspect négatif, réalités positives* (Paris, 1966); J. P. Audet, *Mariage et célibat dans le service pastoral de l'Eglise* (Paris, 1967) (the author shows that obligatory celibacy is tied up with the sacralization of pastoral service between the 2nd and 4th centuries).

[39] So, for example, J. Duquesne, *op. cit.;* I. Illich, *op. cit.;* A. Monjardet, *op. cit.* This total declericalization has been dubbed "declergification" by Marc Oraison.

world? [40] Does the priest's mission oblige him to reintegrate himself fully into the world, or does it oblige him to remain outside the world as a spiritual stimulus? There we have the fundamental cleavage of the present day.

In conclusion we should like to offer two personal observations. As far as priestly celibacy is concerned, it seems to us that there can be no accurate evaluation of the problem while the present obligation is in force. It is only after we get rid of the taboos which survive from an earlier day that we will be able to rediscover the real meaning of the charisms—whatever option we may eventually choose.

Our second observation concerns the priest's professional work. We do not want to overstress the importance of such work, but we would say that if the priest is not adequately integrated into society, this will adversely affect his transmission of the message which is the real goal of his mission. Moreover, these problems will be solved satisfactorily only when we have redefined the respective place of the ministerial priesthood and the common priesthood of the faithful—both on the theoretical and the practical levels. Is it too much to hope that all the members of the Church, laity as well as hierarchy, will have their say on the mission of the priest?

When all is said and done, however, it seems to us that if the priest really wants to discover his precise role, he will have to resign himself to one fact. He will always remain "other" to some extent, not because he is isolated from the world, but because his message plays with fire.

[40] In this direction, for example: J. Laplace, *Le prêtre à la recherche de lui-même* (Paris, 1969); M. Aumont, *Le prêtre: home du sacré* (Paris, 1969); R. Coste, *L'homme-prêtre* (Paris, 1966).

PART III
DOCUMENTATION
CONCILIUM

Office of the Executive Secretary
Nijmegen, Netherlands

Concilium General Secretariat/*Nijmegen, Netherlands*
Josef Smolik/*Prague, Czechoslovakia*

Revolution and Desacralization

Revolution, enlightenment, desacralization and secularization seem to be various phases in an historical process which began in the 19th century and still continues.[1] When the Church is discussed in this connection, one discovers that opinions swing from one extreme to another. Some look on the Church as an institution which much be sacrificed to the revolution like any other antiquated political institution. Others see in the Church the source of all possible revolutions.[2] It is fashionable to take the Church of the first centuries as some kind of norm.[3] The difficulty, however, is that these first centuries belong to the most underdeveloped regions of Church history.[4] And this prompts another question: [5] Is it really so obvious that,

[1] Bibliography in G. Schwaiger, "Das Papsttum im neunzehnten Jahrhundert," in *Hochland* (March-April 1969), pp. 97-112.
[2] O. von Nell-Breuning, "Kirche—Reaktionär oder Revolutionär?" in *Orientierung* 33, 8 (April 30, 1969), pp. 88-90.
[3] Bibliography in J. Knox, *The Early Church and the Coming of the Great Church* (New York, 1955); J. H. Elliot, "The New Testament Is Catholic: A Revaluation of Sola Scriptura," in *Una Sancta* 23, 1 (1966), pp. 3-18; J. Daniélou, "Bulletin d'Histoire des origines chrétiennes," in *Rech. des Sc. Rel.* 57, 1 (Jan./March 1969), pp. 75-130.
[4] J. H. Elliot, "A Catholic Gospel: Reflections on 'Early Catholicism' in the New Testament," in *The Cath. Bibl. Quart.* 31, 2 (April 1969), pp. 213-23.
[5] E. Käsemann, *Exegetische Versuche und Besinnung* I (Göttingen, 1960), pp. 214-23; F. Mussner, " 'Evangelium' und 'Mitte des Evangel-

before 180 A.D., there is such a thing as a "Church"? Is the Gospel not a complex of opposites that can give birth to a movement of dynamic renewal as well as to the static conservatism of a cumbersome body which simply asks for a revolution? [6] It has already often been repeated [7] that the Gospel leaves room for both "left" and "right", and that the universalism of the Church should ensure that in actual reality the Church does not make only one choice out of the many but keeps all possibilities open: the pluriformity of the Church.

In this article we wish to show that (1) revolution is a possibility inherent in the Gospel, and (2) the gospels contain various revolutionary patterns which we ought to reflect upon (theology of revolution). This will show that desacralization is in fact an historical reality but also that neither the revolution nor the "establishment" can be the ultimate reality; the reality of the Church cannot be reduced to either of these two historical movements.

I

REVOLUTION IS A POSSIBILITY INHERENT IN THE GOSPEL

It has frequently been observed that there is not much point in quoting a few isolated texts from the gospels in support of either revolution or the establishment. What matters is to see that the message of the whole Gospel is itself revolutionary. That time

---

iums'," in *Geist in Welt*. I (Freiburg im Br., 1964), pp. 492-514; H. von Campenhausen, *Die Entstehung der christlichen Bibel* (Tübingen, 1968), pp. 1-4.

[6] H. Küng, "Der Frühkatholizismus im Neuen Testament als kontroverstheologisches Problem," in *T.Q.* (1962), pp. 385-442; idem, *Die Kirche* (Freiburg, 1967), p. 125, in which Küng questions whether the attributes attributed to the Church in its earliest days are not rather exaggerated. Judging by its outward appearance and day-to-day activities, to him the Church seems nothing more than a small group of Jews who believed in the Messiah and had their own confession.

[7] Cf. J. H. Elliot (n. 4), p. 219.

has been fulfilled with the coming of Jesus, and this means among other things that we have finished with the kind of life through which man tries to "establish" himself with the help of religion and law; that there is no longer any future for a closed order in which all men and all things were assigned a fixed place and fixed lot; that all must be made new. The real interpretation of the gospels lies in accepting this truth and working it out in life.[8]

It is meaningless to ask whether the authors of the gospels had in mind the kind of revolution we talk about today. As Gadamer pointed out,[9] this credits the authors of the gospels with the wrong kind of quality. Their real achievement lies in the fact that they conveyed such a dynamic message that it surpassed their own understanding. There is an inspiring actuality in the Gospel which constantly asks for renewal. For Churches that have become established institutions, it will always remain difficult to keep up with the driving force of the gospels. They will always have to overcome ther confessionalism. This is one of the reasons why the Catholic Church always refuses to see itself as a "confession"—that is, as one denomination side by side with many other ones. It sees itself as the People of God, constantly and laboriously looking for the answer of faith to the enduring Word of God in the reality of history.[10] This constant effort to listen, as a community, to the Word of God in order to find an historically relevant answer for the present operates against the sacralization of the institution.

This does not mean that the Church is immune from such a sacralization. The articles in this volume rather show the contrary. In this connection Ricoeur talks about a false (because

[8] H. Berger, *De progressieve en de conservatieve mens* (Nijmegen/ Utrecht, 1969), p. 83.
[9] H. G. Gadamer, "Martin Heidegger und die Marburger Theologie," in *Zeit und Geschichte* (Tübingen, 1964), p. 489.
[10] A. Ahlbrecht, "Die Ueberwindung des Konfessionalismus in Theologie und kirchlichem Leben," in *Una Sancta* 20 (1965), pp. 209-15; *idem*, "Konfessionalismus," in *Sacramentum Mundi* III, cols. 2-5 (Freiburg, Basle, Vienna, 1969).

untrue) and a true "scandal" of the Gospel.[11] For him, the false scandal lies in that a Christian would be scandalized by the imposition of a biblical view of the world which can no longer be fitted into the modern view of the world—the sacrifice of his intellect. The true scandal lies in that a Christian can never reduce the message of the Gospel to his present view of the world, and that this, too, must be constantly examined by that practice of the Christian faith to which the inspiration of the Gospel calls him.

If we still can and should read the Gospel, we do so because it has become *our* book. But every new generation will have to make this book its own. In this sense revolution is inherent in the Gospel. It is not a matter of exegesis,[12] but of a growing awareness that the coming of the kingdom of God "from above" presupposes an active encounter "from below". Only where the Christian finds himself in the revolutionary situation will he understand the message of the Gospel as a possibility which can drive him into the border situation of this revolutionary activity. It is in practice that the revolutionary force of the Gospel is discovered. In this sense it has been possible to say [13] that there is no Christian revolution, but there is revolutionary action in Christian responsibility. This means that whatever the Christian achieves under the inspiration of the Gospel will always have a penultimate character because the ultimate, the very heart of his hope, lies always in the active expectation of the kingdom of God, which cannot be manipulated, not even by Christians.

When the revolutionary absolutizes his thought and his deeds, religiously or anti-religiously, the Christian must resist on the ground of that same Gospel. For those who have managed to make the Gospel their own, the experience of the modern world

[11] P. Ricoeur, "Mythe et proclamation chez R. Bultmann," in *Cahiers C.O.P.* 8 (July 1967), esp. p. 28: "Du faux au vrai scandale."

[12] R. Marlé, "Foi et interprétation. Un mot magique: herméneutique," in *Etudes* (May 1969), pp. 669-82.

[13] G. Cruchon, "Ambivalences dans le comportement religieux," in *N. R. Th.* (March 1969), pp. 229-315.

[14] P. Roqueplo, *Expérience du monde: expérience de Dieu* (Paris, 1968), p. 606.

with its urgent problems can lead to the experience of God building his kingdom in this world. They will not see the eschatological realities of the Gospel as an immediate truth but as forcing him to ask in what way it is possible "to stand on the fringe of history" (W. D. Marsch) in our present social conditions.[15] In this sense Marsch considers that the practice of the Christian faith as our response to the message of the Gospel contains already in itself the motivation for a revolutionary awareness. This sounds rather vague, and will be developed in the next section by Josef Smolik.

II
THE THEOLOGY OF REVOLUTION

The Concept of Revolution

Before we can deal with the theology of revolution, we must first have some idea of what revolution means.

The term "revolution" can have many meanings and be used at various levels. Usually, however, it is understood as the violent transfer of the concentration of power from one social class to another that has appeared on the scene. If we wish to analyze this definition further, we have to put the phenomenon of revolution into a wider context. The violent overthrow can only play a positive part when the whole historical situation is already pregnant with this revolutionary state of mind.

This stage, of which violent revolutionary action is the conse-

---

[15] P. A. Stucki, "A propos de l'herméneutique post-bultmannienne," in *Rev. d'Hist. et de Phil. Rel.* I (1969), pp. 33-54.

[16] What follows is a paper read by Josef Smolik in 1968 at a seminar on "Revolution—Idea and Reality," organized by the Catholic and Evangelical Students Association in the monastery of Engelthal. This seminar studied the sociological analysis of various revolutionary patterns and their theological implications: Dr. Werner Post (Bonn), "Phänomen und Typologie der Revolution"; Dr. Krueger (Giessen), "Zur revolutionären Situation in westlichen Industrienationen"; Dr. T. Ebert (Berlin), "Gewaltfreier Aufstand oder revolutionärer Befreiungskrieg".

quence, needs further analysis. *Violent revolution is but a phase in the much wider and deeper revolutionary process.* This process thrives on the search for justice, the opposition to injustice and the irresistible urge toward human freedom. The *motivation of this revolutionary attitude* does not rest primarily on the degree of oppression the people are suffering. The history of the 19th century shows that in many cases people saw their misery as something inevitable and did not realize that this misery was caused by oppression. The true motivation of revolutionary resistance must be looked for in man's inner attitude. Man becomes aware of his dignity, begins to notice injustice and oppression, and so reaches the *conviction that the situation can and must be altered.*

Where does this revolutionary spirit come from? The answer to this question leads us to various revolutionary traditions which can be found in all European nations.

The revolutionary process in the various nations always shows a direct connection with revolutionary traditions which have remained alive for centuries in the consciousness of the people.

This revolutionary process, which discovers and is inspired by the dynamic elements in history, looks toward a *future eschatological horizon.* Every revolutionary process entails *a vision of the future,* a new pattern which is formulated into a program. In this sense futurology is a revolutionary science.

Within this revolutionary process the matter of a violent overthrow is a most important question, yet neither the only one, nor even the central one. The revolutionary process necessarily brings with it the struggle for power. And this leads to the question of revolutionary strategy so that power can be transferred effectively.

The New Testament Background

The New Testament can give us some theological orientation in the ambiguities and tensions of the revolutionary process.

1. *The Synoptics.* Biblical scholars tell us that it is impossible

to extract a biography of Jesus of Nazareth from the gospels. Nevertheless, they are inclined to accept that there are certain points in these narratives that are historically reliable. One of these points is the extraordinary sovereign authority of Jesus which allowed him to reduce that of Moses and the law. As E. Käsemann says: "This sovereign authority not only shook the foundations of later Judaism and was therefore a decisive factor in bringing about Jesus' death, but, beyond that, also revolutionized the philosophy of life of antiquity with its opposition of sacred and secular and its demonology." [17]

The second feature of Jesus' personality which is historically wholly reliable is his solidarity with sinners, the godless and those discriminated against. H. Braun particularly has drawn attention to this basic attitude of Jesus. It is true that Bultmann does not accept the historical Jesus of Nazareth as theologically significant, but his followers begin to recognize that the historical Jesus is theologically important.

It is certainly not mere accident that precisely these two features, historically accepted even by Bultmann's disciples, contain revolutionary motives and are theologically important. It is precisely in the persistence of these motives that Jesus sees the sign of the presence of the kingdom of God. The kingdom of God, which flows into time through the person of Jesus, is described as an eschatological reality by biblical scholars. We can go farther and see in this kingdom of God *a revolutionary reality*. Whenever the reality of the kingdom of God appears in the gospels, the ecclesiastical or political sacralized *status quo* is deprived of power, and something wholly unexpected and new happens which confounds the guardians of order and has a revolutionary effect. The revolutionary process, which Jesus unleashed through his vision of God's kingdom in connection with the revolutionary events in the Old Testament, offended the established power, first of the Sanhedrin and then of Rome. The

---

[17] E. Käsemann, "Das Problem des historischen Jesus," in *Exegetische Versuche und Besinnungen* I (Göttingen, 1960), p. 208.

opposition to Jesus of Nazareth increased until it began to make *use of violence* in order to arrest the whole revolutionary process. In spite of this tension Jesus refused to give up the struggle for the kingdom of God. He refused to make common cause with those revolutionary groups that identified the kingdom of God with the political freedom of Israel and considered violence the only legitimate means in this struggle for freedom. He saw to it that his public gatherings were not politically twisted. In his struggle for the kingdom of God Jesus excluded any compromise with violence. The groups of nationalists and terrorists who opposed Rome and the violence of a Sanhedrin which leaned on Rome never were potential allies in his eyes.

While Jesus refused to give up the struggle, he also refused to have the methods of the freedom fighters or of the counterrevolutionaries imposed upon him. Jesus followed the path of *total non-violence* and excluded every kind of pressure, even that of passive resistance. He did not gather around him large masses of people who would deprive him forcibly of his freedom to follow his own way. (The only exception is the entry into Jerusalem, but this should be carefully interpreted.)

Jesus remained wholly faithful to his "vision" of the kingdom, both in method and in content, and did not allow the secular vision of national freedom to turn him away from his purpose.

We can sum up the synoptic contribution to the question of revolution in the following points:

a. The central idea of Jesus' message, *the notion of the kingdom of God, contains revolutionary elements.*

b. These revolutionary elements in the kingdom of God can be specified as the *irreconcilable resistance to any sacralization of the reality (the struggle against the law) and to any discrimination against human beings.*

c. The revolutionary elements in the kingdom of God represent a theological and *pre-political phase in the revolutionary process.* The fight against the sacralization of the law is a theological idea, and only when applied does it have consequences

for the ecclesiastical institutional and even political situation.
Jesus' solidarity with the godless transcends the political front,
even in the battle for freedom. In his own circle Jesus certainly
had some former members of the freedom fighters, "zealots" as
they were called (e.g., Simon Zelotes), but at the human level
he did not reject those that actually represented Roman milita-
rism and imperialism (Mt. 8) or their collaborators. *The revolution of the kingdom of God is so profoundly and totally human*
that it must be described as pre-political and theological.

d. *These* theological and *pre-political elements* of the revolutionary process of the kingdom of God *must remain recognizable*
even in the revolutionary situation of power politics, *for the sake
of the value of life.* Only in this way can we enforce the rights of
freedom and the future.

e. The overthrow of power politics can never be by itself the
final solution. The *pre-political,* theological *elements of the kingdom do not allow for a glorification of such an overthrow.*

2. *St. Paul.* Paul continued the theological, pre-political revolution of Jesus in his struggle for freedom from the law. In this
way he opened the door to the Gentiles and could make the Gospel intelligible to Hellenism. In this revolutionary struggle with
the Jews and the Jewish Christians, a tense situation was created
where the Jews made use of power-political means. In his defense
Paul did not limit himself to theology and non-violence. He
claimed his Roman citizenship and appealed to the laws of the
Roman Empire. He did not gamble with political power but, in
contrast to Jesus, did not hesitate to use this existing power in
his defense. And thus the question of State law entered into the
revolutionary process of early Christianity.

Paul's second front was his fight against the *spiritual enthusi-
asts* who can be described as theological anarchists. These en-
thusiasts had so little respect for all political structures that in
their theology they refused to recognize the existence and importance of these structures. Paul rejected this early Christian
anarchism. Romans 13 should be understood in this context. The

text has nothing to do with a sacralization of the State but with the fact that, in this "interim" existence, *the kingdom of God on earth lives in a dubious symbiosis with those power structures* and will have to go on living with them *until the parousia,* the coming of the Lord. And in this existence these structures have not only a negative but also *a positive part* to play. Paul recognizes this fact and uses it in his struggle with the Jews.

Paul is often interpreted as *supporting conservative theology.* This is due to the fact that conservative theology has no understanding for the importance of the *parousia* and the eschatological elements in Paul's thought. When one takes these elements out of his thought, his statements have a conservative ring about them which is totally opposed to his real mind. This can be seen in the question of *slavery.* His words that each should be content with his place in society is made to serve as proof that Paul was *in social matters a conservative.* But if we put these words in their full context, we cannot exclude the eschatological background. Paul's interest in the social order was basically weakened by his expectation of the *parousia* as almost on the doorstep. But this weakening of interest can hardly be seen as a sacralization of the *status quo* in this eschatological context. It is precisely this *status quo* which Paul refuses to recognize in the light of the *parousia* ("because the world as we know it is passing away": 1 Cor. 7, 31).

We can sum up Paul's "theology of the revolution" as follows:

a. Paul worked out the theology of the revolutionary elements of the Synoptics and applied them in the life of the Church.

b. The first revolutionary element is *the attitude toward the law.* His teaching of "grace alone" and "faith alone" rejected any sacralization of the law and the Jewish tradition.

c. The second revolutionary element in Paul is his fight against any form of discrimination, with its emphasis on the universalism of the Gospel.

d. What is new in Paul is the explicit and positive attitude toward the power structures. The revolutionary process can, in its theological, pre-political phase, appeal to State law in the case of an ultimate threat.

e. We judge the positive function of the State in this existence (*aeon*) by its structure, principles and content, but this judgment is historically conditioned.

3. *St. John*. Insofar as the understanding of the pre-political phase of the revolutionary process is concerned, John barely differs from the Synoptics. But the confrontation of this process with the Jews and Pilate is dealt with in greater theological detail. John put the pre-political revolutionary stirrings which provoked Jesus to action, in a broader international political perspective. The Sanhedrin, which tried to defend the small Jewish nation against the imperialistic super-power of Rome, feared that Jesus' activities would provoke reprisals and military intervention. That is why they interpreted the execution of Jesus as a political act: in order to save the people. In a small nation which could endanger itself and the whole world by some revolutionary activity, one could not tolerate any pre-political revolutionary process. John throws more light on *the conflicts between Jesus and the Jews*. It is here a question of *total revolution within the nation of Israel*. The Jews whose father is Beelzebub usurped the place of God. A total revolution must restore the God of truth to his place in Israel.

Johannine theology shows a new development in the book of Revelation. There Rome appears as the beast from the abyss, the "Antichrist", and "Christian freedom is unmistakably linked with a political revolutionary attitude".[18] Käsemann has drawn attention to the special type of revolutionary as described in the book of Revelation: "They do not fight to acquire power, but because they must become like unto the Lord. They do not want to conquer the world, but to defend the Lord's claim on the earth, and they are ready to die for this. Their aim is not the overthrow of the existing order but to bear witness to the fact that he, who makes all things new, is on his way. They

[18] *Idem, Der Ruf der Freiheit* (Tübingen, ²1968), p. 133.

simply act as deputies for the creator in a fallen world, and therefore have to concern themselves with those that have set themselves up in their own name over against the Lord; such people do not understand power as simply a mandate of the Lord, and so abuse it. As such, the Christians who accept the call to resistance are not only witnesses to God's sovereignty and signs of its reality, but at the same time represent a misused creation, and speak up for all those who are oppressed. Egypt, the people of the desert, which everybody sees around him, must finally be behind, and only the *exodus* can bring salvation." [19]

The book of Revelation represents a new phase. The pre-political phase is left behind and we enter the revolutionary arena. To resist demoniacal power is the only possible attitude a Christian can adopt. But it is a revolutionary attitude of solidarity with all those who are oppressed and discriminated against.

The New Testament shows such a rich variety of attitudes that it is impossible to derive a fundamental ethic from it.

4. *Three patterns of Christian existence contained in the New Testament.* I have tried to show that, within this variety of attitudes, we can discern three patterns of "social existence" for the Christian and the Church:

a. *The pre-political (but not a-political)* attitude which operates at the level of the universally human. This pre-political attitude has its roots in the Gospel. It implies a revolutionary tendency and adopts a critical attitude toward Church and society. It has a powerful appeal because of its inner truth. This revolutionary stirring is not politically motivated, but has nevertheless important political consequences. It is not afraid of these consequences, nor does it misuse them. It therefore always incarnates the sign of the cross.

b. *The conservative pattern.* Here the initial revolutionary stirrings pass into a revolutionary movement. The revolutionary movement of Christians does not hesitate to appeal to legal guarantees in the expectation that the State will correctly deal with the positive forces of the Christian movement. This revolu-

[19] *Ibid.,* p. 146.

tion operates in the field of theology and of the individual man within the Christian community.

c. *The revolutionary pattern*. In the historical situation of a sacralized and mystified State, which leads to oppression and injustice, the Christian adopts a radical revolutionary line in direct opposition to the mystified violence of the State.

None of these patterns can be held up as normative for the Christian. The individual Christian must make up his own mind within the concrete historical situation. Up until now the life of the Church has been dominated by the first two patterns in various combinations, while the revolutionary pattern has been neglected. There have been whole periods in the history of Christianity where the power of the State or the pope was mystified without any revolutionary reaction on the part of the Christians. When they did so, on theological (J. Hus) [20] or scientific (Galileo) grounds, the Church did not reform itself but simply ruled out the possibility of revolution as incompatible with Christianity, ready to make use of penal laws and actual penalization if necessary, regardless of the fact whether the Church was of the Catholic or the Protestant variety. And so the revolutionary pattern needs to be theologically rediscovered in the New Testament, not only in the book of Revelation but also in the pre-political pattern of the Synoptics and St. John.

Systematic Observations

1. *The eschatological view of reality*. The biblical view of reality is eschatological. Eschatology sees reality as dynamic, open to the future. This reality is therefore liable to change, not only in the anthropological field, but in its totality. This kind of reality can be expressed by the word "process". In spite of its plasticity, its changeability, biblical reality must be understood as real. It is meant to achieve a purpose. This meaning of reality is not obvious but emerges from revelation in Jesus Christ. This revelation is therefore the source of the dynamic quality of reality.

2. *The "ontocratic" view of reality*. In the Bible the

eschatological view of reality is confronted with another view which Arend van Leeuwen [21] called "ontocratic". This means that reality is seen as the overriding "order", as hierarchically structured, and by nature static. Insofar as movement appears in this reality, it is only a cyclic movement which does not turn reality into something dynamic but rather locks it in a stable situation of eternally closed circles. This view of reality is based on power, and this power is seen as the sacralized theological source of stability. This kind of "realism" is highly allergic to any movement that crosses its circular path and wants to break out in pursuit of a purpose. In such a system every change is, so to speak, seismographically observed and interpreted as an indication of chaos. All pre-Christian systems were imbued with this view. It found its philosophical expression in Aristotelianism. In this view history is meaningless.

3. *The conflict between these two views.* The history of the Christian Church shows that the conflict between these two views is of long standing. While the energy of early Christianity was inspired by its eschatological vision, the "ontocratic" had already slipped into theological thought before Constantine, and became prevalent after him. The Reformation and the various modern revolutions shattered this "ontocratic" Aristotelian pattern and led to a new situation. The theological situation today is marked by the conflict between the shattered "ontocratic" position and a theological trend inspired by history and eschatology. The point at issue is whether theology can cope with the external dynamics of reality unleashed by the technological revolution. The theological problem of revolution arises precisely there where the eschatological reality emerges and where the "ontocratic" structures try to control it by their own kind of legalism and to force it into the "ontocratic" *status quo.*

4. *The revolutionary reality.* The theological problem of revolution as well as the problem of revolution at large consists

[20] The case of the Waldensians in connection with this point has been dealt with in an historical study by K. V. Selge, *Die ersten Waldenser.*
[21] A. T. van Leeuwen, *Christianity in World History* (London, 1964).

in preventing this kind of integration and in remaining faithful to the eschatological, revolutionary reality. We have to prevent the revolutionary reality from turning into a utopia [22] or an apocalyptic vision. The difference between utopia and genuine revolution lies in that utopia is so far away from reality that it becomes an illusion. It is not radical enough because it does not start at the root of reality; it is unrealistic.

5. *Revolutionary awareness.* Revolutionary awareness is built up in small circles within or, most frequently, outside the institutional Church. It breaks through wherever man becomes aware of his humanity and shakes off the shackles of the power fetish. It cannot break through where power and the laws of power constitute the final argument. The heart of the revolutionary reality is the freedom from all power and its laws, a freedom which Jesus asserted before Pilate. Revolutionary awareness links up with historical traditions and is nourished by them. I wish to stress that the Christian tradition, correctly interpreted, shows itself to be a source of revolutionary awareness. We misinterpret the New Testament when we do not encourage this revolutionary awareness in historical situations where power is totally misused.

6. *Revolutionary program and strategy.* The revolutionary awareness of the Christian and that of the Marxist are at one insofar as both are opposed to the sacralization of the *status quo.* The dialogue between the two starts at the point where the revolutionary reality raises the question of the use of power. At present there is a tension between the program of revolution, to which a Christian subscribes, and the strategy of revolution, which raises the issue of violence. The danger here lies in stressing the question of strategy at the expense of the program. The result will then be that, once power has been taken over, the program is in danger of losing its intrinsic appeal because it is only used to guarantee the newly acquired power. This will lead to a hypertrophy of power, so that power may well come to

[22] Cf. the article on "Utopia" in *Concilium* 41 (1969), pp. 149-65.

178 CONCILIUM GENERAL SECRETARIAT AND JOSEF SMOLIK

bury the program of revolution, and revolution to bury itself. In this context one may wonder whether it might not be *the Christian's specific contribution to revolution* to hold on to the original program and its motivation. There is really a genuine danger that revolution will betray itself and lose its integrity by not remaining faithful to itself. A revolution needs a conscience. Without a conscience the revolutionary overthrow will turn into a dictatorship which ends in terrorism.

7. *The revolutionary conscience.* Who must be the conscience of revolution? The Church failed to be the conscience of the feudal overlords. Because of her nervous fear of revolution, she cannot play that part today either. And yet, I think it is the duty of a Christian to commit himself to humanistic revolutionary programs, to cooperate with the revolutionaries, even when they aim at a violent overthrow of the establishment, and to render them the service of being their conscience. This may lead, in the case of a successful revolution, to the risk of being misunderstood and considered either a counter-revolutionary or a revolutionary on the part of those who have the power. This is obvious. That this risk may lead one to the gallows has been shown by Jesus. The "Zealots", Judas probably among them, thought he was a counter-revolutionary; Pilate, beset by Jewish pressures, saw him as a nationalistic freedom fighter, and in fact he so died. The specific Christian and risky contribution to revolution consists in the defense of the *human* program of revolution against its violent contraction both before and particularly after revolution, and he will respect the tactics of revolution as long as it does not become an end in itself.[23]

[23] R. A. McCormick, "The Theology of Revolution," in *Theol. Studies* 29, 4 (Dec. 1968), pp. 685-97; W. Schweitzer, "Die 'Theologie der Revolution'," in *Evang. Ethik* 12, 3 (May 1968), pp. 174-81; M. M. Thomas, "Issues Concerning the Life and Work of the Church in a Revolutionary World," in *The Ecum. Review* 20, 4 (Oct. 1968), pp. 410-19; *Eglise et Société: La responsabilité des gouvernments à une époque révolutionnaire* (Geneva, 1966), p. 267; "Revolution und Theologie. Das neue in unsere Zeitalter. Ein Symposon," in *Frankfurter Hefte* 22, 9 (1967), pp. 161-30.

But where it does become an end in itself, where revolution is glorified as such, he must oppose it in the name of the revolutionary program. This means that he remains a revolutionary, when the others have turned into bureaucrats and strategists.

BIOGRAPHICAL NOTES

LEONARDUS LAEYENDECKER: Born in the Netherlands in 1930, he studied theology, and then social science, at the University of Amsterdam, receiving his doctorate in sociology in 1967. He is a member of the Faculty of Social Science at the University of Amsterdam, and the author of various articles on religious sociology.

HENRICUS FORTMANN: Born in the Netherlands in 1912, he was ordained in 1936. He studied at the University of Nijmegen, receiving his doctorate in psychology. A professor of religion and of comparative psychology, his published works include the four-volume *Als ziende de Onzienlijk* (Hilversum, 1964-68), and *Geistige Gesundheit und religiöses Leben* (Vienna, 1968).

GEORGE EVERY: Born in England in 1909, he is an Anglican and a member of the Society of the Sacred Mission. He studied at Kelham Theological College, receiving his B.A. in history and the arts. He is associate editor of *Theoria to Theory,* and literary editor of the *Eastern Churches Review.* His published works include *The Byzantine Patriarchate* (London, 1962), and *Misunderstandings between East and West* (London, 1965).

MICHEL MESLIN: Born in Paris in 1926, he is a Catholic. He holds a teaching diploma and a doctorate in literature, and is dean of studies of the Faculty of Literature in Rennes. His published works include *Les Ariens d'Occident* (Paris, 1967), and currently in preparation is *La fête des Kalendes de janvier dans l'Empire romain.*

YVES CONGAR, O.P.: Born in France in 1904, he was ordained in 1930. He studied at the Catholic Institute in Paris and at the Saulchoir, receiving degrees in literature, philosophy and theology. He has recently published *L'Ecclésiologie du Haut Moyen-Age* and a new edition of *Vraie et fausse réforme dans l'Eglise.* He is editor of the period from St. Augustine to the present day in *L'Histoire des doctrines ecclesiologiques* in the Dogmengeschichte series. In addition, he is both founder and director of the series *Unam Sanctam,* in which, together with a number of distinguished collaborators, he has published extensive commentaries on Vatican Council II.

181

HANS BORNEWASSER: Born in the Netherlands in 1924, he is a Catholic. He studied at the University of Nijmegen, receiving doctorates in philosophy and literature. He is professor of Church history at the theological faculty of Tilburg, president of the Nederlands Historisch Genootschap and editor of *Archief voor de Geschiedenis van de katholieke Kerk in Nederland*. His publications include *50 jaar katholieke leergangen* (Tilburg, 1962).

ENRIQUE DUSSEL: Born in Argentina in 1934, he is a Catholic. He studied in Argentina at the National University of Cuyo, and in Europe at Louvain, Mainz, Münster, Madrid, and in Paris at the Sorbonne and the Catholic Institute. He holds doctorates in philosophy and literature and a licentiate in theology. He is professor of philosophical anthropology at the National University of Cuyo and at the University College of Anthropology of Mendoza. His published works include *Hipótesis para una historia de la Iglesia en América latina* (Barcelona, 1967), and *El protestantismo en América latina* (Fribourg, 1967).

JOSEPH COMBLIN: Born in Brussels in 1923, he was ordained in 1947. He studied at Louvain, receiving his doctorate in theology in 1953. He is professor of theology at the regional seminary of Recife in Brazil. His publications include the three-volume *Theologie de la Paix* (Paris, 1963-66), and *Le Christ dans l'Apocalypse* (Paris, 1965).

IRÉNÉE-HENRI DALMAIS, O.P.: Born in France in 1914, he was ordained in 1945. He studied at the Saulchoir, at the University of Lyons, and at the Sorbonne. He holds degrees in literature, philosophy and theology, and is professor of Oriental liturgy at the Higher Institute of Liturgy in Paris. His published works include *Initiation à la Liturgie* (Paris, 1958), *Eastern Liturgies* (London, 1960), and *Saints et sanctuaires d'Orient* (Paris, 1968).

DOMINIQUE JULIA: Born in France in 1940, he is a Catholic. He studied at the Sorbonne, receiving his teaching diploma in history in 1964. Since 1965 he has been assistant lecturer of modern and contemporary history at the Sorbonne. He is the author of numerous articles on history and religious sociology.

WILLEM FRIJHOFF: Born in the Netherlands in 1942, he was ordained in 1966. He studied philosophy and theology in the Netherlands, and is now continuing his studies at the Faculty of Literature in Paris.

JOSEF SMOLIK: Born in Czechoslovakia in 1922, he was ordained in the Evangelical Church of Bohemian Brothers in 1946. He studied at the Faculty of Theology in Prague, and at the Union Theological Seminary, New York. He received his doctorate in theology, and since 1966 has been professor of pastoral theology in Prague. His published works include *Die Predigt in der Reformation* (Prague, 1957), and *Gegenwärtige Versuche um die Interpretation des Evangeliums* (Prague, 1968).